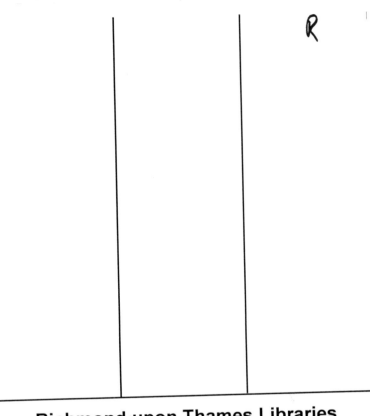

R

Richmond upon Thames Libraries

Renew online at www.richmond.gov.uk/libraries

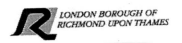
LONDON BOROUGH OF
RICHMOND UPON THAMES

Nine Rules to Conquer Death

Nine Rules
to Conquer Death

KEVIN TOOLIS

ONEWORLD

A Oneworld Book

First published in Great Britain, the Republic of Ireland
and Australia by Oneworld Publications, 2020

ISBN 978-1-78607-983-1
eISBN 978-1-78607-984-8

Typeset by Hewer Text UK Ltd, Edinburgh
Printed and bound in Great Britain by Clays Ltd, Elcograf S.p.A.

Oneworld Publications
10 Bloomsbury Street
London WC1B 3SR
England

Stay up to date with the latest books,
special offers, and exclusive content from
Oneworld with our newsletter

Sign up on our website
oneworld-publications.com

MIX
Paper from
responsible sources
FSC® C018072

Nine Rules to Conquer Death

How should we conquer death?

Our eternal existential question. The unspoken *why* of all action and thought.

Death is our silenced paradox. All around us but the unseen.

A shadow companion who haunts our gnawing anxieties over what is to become of us, sometimes even in the smallest details.

The virus.

The stab of doubt in every lump beneath the skin.

That sneezing stranger on the other side of the aisle.

The phone call far too late in the night to be anything but disaster.

Your cough.

The word, fresh from a day's distance, that your father, your mother, has taken a turn and an ambulance is at the door.

The right-hand turn across the bristling incoming traffic.

A jolt of panic at your own table, choking over a trapped morsel of dry bread, when you suddenly can't breathe.

That unexplained dull fatigue.

Or the would-be rupture in the universe; the lost or absent wayward child, their phone ringing out, the fearful edge, that tears through your heart.

The awful realisation.

Is this the moment when I die?

Catastrophe begins.

Bracing yourself already for the worst?

———

Can anyone overcome their fear of dying? Or conquer death?

Even the question seems so overwhelming. What's the point?

Surely it's better just to never talk about death at all? Deny death and say nothing? Turn the volume down. Flip the picture's face against the wall and just keep on going on with the rest of our lives and pretend by never mentioning the D-word out loud.

Or hide behind silly euphemisms like 'passed' or 'passing'.

Lying to ourselves. Silencing our private thoughts. Even in the panic of a viral pandemic.

Barricading our fear in the mind-numbing white noise of whatever screen devours us.

Filling up our days with the antics of so-called celebrities. Soap stars. Movie stars. Social media 'stars'.

Proceedings to beguile time.

Tuning in to talk shows that talk and talk, round and round, about – nothing. Or nothing important enough to be remembered the day after.

Watching the same films, the same plots, the same 'stars', that look and sound the same because they are the same thing wrapped up in another name.

Listening to the radio blur of a thousand headlines, the chirpy upbeat studio hosts, in between the tyre adverts, the dedication calls, reports of traffic snarls and the weather.

The tip and tap of Twitter, Facebook, TikTok, Snapchat or Something Else bleeding out our life minutes into the digital wilderness.

Distractions in the lonesome search for affirmation.

Hanging around on the side benches of our lives, lingering our way towards oblivion. One day closer to extinction.

Gamers.

Which is a pretty accurate summary of where we are with death right now in the Western world.

Until the day when real death comes anyway, the screen shatters into pieces, and you find yourself alone, defenceless in this mortal world.

What then?

What do we do with ourselves then?

Supposing we tried to do death in a different way?

An older way?

How about we go out and conquer death first?

––––––––––

Can't be that hard, can it?

We spend a lot of our lives training and practising lots of different skill sets.

How to control our bodies.

How to walk, speak, ride a bike, study, date, diet, parent a child or become a better person.

We fill up our days with classes, seminars, books and how-to-does on every human activity from cooking to astrology. Yoga and baking bread.

We study technical manuals, download apps, go to conventions and follow rules all the time until we achieve mastery of the subject.

Physics, Maths, French.

So why can't we do the same with death?

Sign up for a how-to-die course where we learn all the rules, do a few tests, practise again and again and get better at dying? Pass the exam.

Do you think that is ridiculous?

Because dying is a totally different thing?

It's the end? No ifs or buts.
You just die alone and that's it.
Why would anyone ever want to learn about dying?
What is the point? Or to even think about death?
How could you teach anyone how to die?
I, you, us, we want to live not die.

———————

There are two simple but profound answers to the how-to-die question. The first answer is that even if you don't want to do the course it's compulsory. Dying.

You still have to turn up on exam day. Virus or no virus. So you don't really have a choice. Each of us has somehow got to find a way to work out some sort of personal plan with death. And there is another important thing.

Far from being a unique once-at-the-end-of-your-life-time event, death is an every-other-day commonplace.

People die around us all the time, those we love, our wider family and community, the strangers we hear and see in the newspapers or on the TV. So death is not just about you or me.

Dying happens to everyone, everywhere, sometime. Not just in pandemics. Cancer, heart attacks, car crashes, suicides are just as lethal too. Plain old-fashioned mortalities.

We all have to find a way too to navigate ourselves around the deaths of others.

What if we did death the same way we practise for any other human activity – like how we learn to drive a car – by taking lessons? Surely dying would become easier too?

Does it sound too simple an answer? A trick question?

But just as no one sane would get in a car and head out for the nearest motorway without first knowing how to drive, so surely it is equally foolish to believe you can live all your life without understanding the basic rules of human mortality?

The rules? What rules? Are there any?

Yes. There are rules because the second answer is that for all of human history our ancestors have practised learning how to conquer death every day of their lives by sharing the company of the dying, touching the bodies of the dead and going to wakes and funerals.

Which is what the ancient Greeks, the Romans, the Etruscans, the Aztecs, the Vikings, Africans, Asians, Europeans and the Celts did. And what the Irish still do in the Irish Wake.

Death was no stranger nor a great mystery. You learned how to die by seeing other people die right in front of you, sometimes badly and sometimes peacefully.

Wakes and funerals were part of everyday life and parents taught their children how to die by bringing them along to see the dead themselves and get a feel, literally the touch of a corpse, of what death was like.

Our ancestors had a whole set of death-conquering rules they followed and they had a lot of fun too: wailing, grieving out loud, feasting, drinking, reminiscing, story-telling, staying up all night, flirting or *prumsaí,* as they say in Irish, and even having sex at funerals.

The dead, the dying, the living and their community were bound together in a web of ritual and reverence that stretched beyond the grave and made sense of their universe.

They conquered death together.

In the Western world, we've lost that communal wisdom. We are far too sad about death for our own good. Too scared. Too often we think of our own death like the death of the sun; all the light and planets of the galaxy, the known universe, will die with us. So what's the point?

Modern death has become a personally terrifying experience; an 'I' death never a 'we' death. An unremitting tragedy that we will all face alone. Extinction.

Too sad for our own good? How can you not be sad about dying? Or too scared about your own death? The coronavirus? The thousands and thousands of people who died for no good reason?

Well part of the reason why we are so scared is we are getting death all wrong.

We have never been taught how to face death openly in the first place. Or how to grieve.

No one hands out the guidelines, the manual, any more. Or tells us what death is like. There are no death education classes on the school curriculum . No 'teach-ins' on the mortal routine of what happens when people die. No practice papers for what to say to the dying, the bereaved.

Or how to die ourselves.

Which is a bit strange when you think about how important death is. And how present dying is in our daily lives. How we think about the possibilities of dying, almost hourly, when we are near a road, an electrical socket, a cliff, climbing stairs or eating biscuits.

How many times have you thought about dying already today? Like avoiding being knocked down by that oncoming truck? Or not falling into that basement? Or not being poisoned by the out-of-date chicken breasts in the fridge? The cough that could be the sign of something lurking within your own body?

Our new way of meeting death is like being thrown into the driver's seat of a strange moving rental car not knowing where we are going and just being told to drive even when we don't recognise any of the controls. Like how the gears work. Or where the indicators are rather than the windscreen wipers.

Even as the car speeds up each of us has to individually rediscover death all on our own just as we are being whooshed along a dark, spooky unknown road marked Oblivion. It's hard not to panic, calm our fear, or feel uniquely singled out.

We have lost the rulebook, the guidebook, on our own mortality.

Instead we have become conquered by death.

But there is another way.

In theory, we should never be happier about dying. We have it made. Compared to our predecessors we live lives of both unimaginable luxury and longevity.

In 1800 there were a billion humans on the planet, the vast majority of whom lived in extreme poverty. Most children died in infancy. Polluted water, starvation and myriad diseases, smallpox, cholera, malaria, syphilis, bubonic plague, ravaged the population. Tuberculosis alone killed one in four.

The average life expectancy was forty.

Today there are 7.7 billion humans and global life expectancy is 71.5 years even with the virus.

If you were born in the rich part of the world then you will probably live well into your eighties.

We are better fed, better educated, taller, healthier and through medical science have access to an extraordinary range of drugs and tools to enable us to lead far more productive, longer, pain-free lives.

Our death, you would think, should be easier to handle. We should all be far more reconciled in general to dying painlessly in a gentle morphine fog, surrounded by medical professionals, at the end of our attenuated days. Even in a viral pandemic.

Of course, that's not the point, is it? A lot of old dead folks? History. My death is a me question. What happens to me. My life. My family. Why should I care about all those strangers? Those Others?

The nightly death toll of Covid-19 victims. The drip, drip of casualties, shootings, traffic pile-ups, on the evening news. The starving children, the blasted cities, the fleeing refugees, of foreign lands. The neighbourhood chatter of cancer deaths, coronaries and the lingering dementias of friends' parents.

Their deaths have got nothing to do with me. Or my death. I just don't want ME to die.

But the My-Death-versus-the-Other question just brings you back into the same silenced death paradox.

The more we seemingly distance ourselves from death the greater our own fear. The more we recoil from the Other, the sick, the dying, and death in our daily lives in the West, the more anxious we become about ourselves. More scared. More unreconciled to our own nature.

Now we worry about dying four or five times a day but never feel able to share our fears out loud. The terror of the virus-laden supermarket trolley handle, the suicidal thoughts, the sense of everything failing, losing everything you've ever loved, your anger over what will never be and your death loneliness.

Loneliness?

Well when did you last have a proper conversation about dying? Or ever? Even in the viral panic. Talk about your fear?

Now, we are not sure where to place ourselves against these Others, the dying, the nameless dead and the bereaved.

What to say to the afflicted? Or how to comfort the bereaved. Or find the right way to express the sadness we feel. Or even how to behave at the few funerals we go to.

We are even scared to teach children about dying, worrying we will frighten them to death by letting them in on our Grim Reaper secret that one day they will die too?

Inside ourselves we are no longer sure how to negotiate our own mortality.

Our ancestors, who constantly faced random death and inexplicable disease, would be ashamed of our death cowardice.

———

Our mortality is now a tragedy not an act of nature.

The death of a child we deem an offence against natural order, a crime, which no parent should ever face when for most of our species' history every parent before us lost several if not most of their children to illness. Just as millions of children in poor countries still die of disease today.

Perversely, until the coronavirus pandemic, our conception of plague, our biological vulnerability, became so remote that up to ten percent of parents in Western society refused to inoculate their children against potentially lethal viruses like measles because such a way of dying, contagion, had become inconceivable to them. And some individuals still do believe vaccines are the control mechanisms of some malign global conspiracy.

For others the pandemic has shattered generations of denial and death complacency and given us all a glimpse of the worlds of plague and terror our ancestors lived through.

Seduced by a mythic certainty of distant old-age expiration, we were for far too long bewildered by death's random compulsion in ending the lives of the young and early-middle-aged.

A Celestial Sniper who picks off victims for no fathomable reason and ruptures the logic of the universe with inexplicable viral succumbings, childhood leukaemias, accidents on park swings, school shootings, teenage suicides, brides with bowel cancer, non-smokers with lung tumours, and traffic collisions.

A Never-Should-Have-Been, an injustice, we cannot fully explain to ourselves because death is such a purposeless unnatural loss.

We resent death yet feel uniquely vulnerable, traumatised, angry and often seek something, or someone, to blame because in a Better World such tragedies should never happen. We want an explanation, a reason, a cause, a why.

'No one, no family, should ever have to experience what we have gone through,' runs as a common refrain in the interviews of the grieving relatives on television even when what has been gone through, although sad, is a repeat mortal commonality: a lost child, a civic failing, an act of terrorist murder, even plagues.

Strangest of all, in some instances, we have conferred on death a celebrity status. Dying of cancer, or even dying itself, is written up as if mortality was an untoward challenge, an optional personal quest on Everest, that must be memorialised for its unique insights by the most adventurous among us rather than a common tale of expiry on the universal road. Many of these individual stories are written and blogged about with grace and courage and have great value. But why is there a need for them to be written at all? Was nothing ever passed down in our own lives along with those familiar childhood fairy stories? *Goodnight Moon* and *Goodnight Death*? Or, *We're Going on a Death Hunt*?

Did no one we know, a granny, an uncle, ever die before in the usual order of things? Or show us where the real Wild Things hang out in the local graveyard? Why has no one in the family or school, even work, ever taught us about dying before?

Where did our new fairy tale '*We Will Never Die*' begin?

Why do we need to rediscover death at all?

———————

Grief has become our private purgatory.

We have abandoned the rites of public mourning but are surprised when grief becomes our mental prison and we are haunted by our unquiet dead.

Instead of a public wake or a black armband we carry around inside ourselves a secret graveyard for the souls of those we have loved but can never truly bury because we have lost a public space to wail and keen and grieve out our loss.

We live on in a death-silenced world yet our unexpurgated grief when it inevitably erupts out, we feel, is longer-lasting, more corrosive, easily carried over into a medically defined traumatic stress disorder. A sickness caused by death that must be addressed by therapies, workshops, trauma classes and self-help manuals.

Sadly, if that is the appropriate word, we miss out on all the fun in death. When my 90-year-old Aunt Mary died on the remote Irish island where all my family are from, we had a great time.

Aside from her children, dozens of her nieces and nephews flew back from all parts of the world to be there at her wake, honour her and hold a great party. Hundreds of people came to see her in her coffin and say goodbye. There were tears, but there was also a lot of joy, pride in the substitute mother she had been for so many of us summer after summer when we were children, and joy too in the gathering of this whole clan to celebrate the end of her life. My Aunt Mary was there too at her funeral because we could see her, touch her, even kiss her, in her open coffin.

And then we buried her and got on with the rest of our lives.

———

Our heightened Western personal death anxiety runs in tandem with a recently acquired prohibition on the sight of the dead in a Western Death Machine that medicalises and controls every aspect of the dying process.

A Whisper Death World where it is more common than uncommon to have never seen, let alone touched, a dead human in your entire life.

Western Death Machine?

Whisper Death World?

'Western Death Machine' is just a kind of shorthand to describe the complex historical process over the last two hundred years by which we have handed over the control of our mortality to professional intermediaries like doctors and undertakers, pallbearers, gravediggers and the state. We have screened ourselves away from the sick, the dying and the dead as if such happenings belong to another world apart from our own. We have abandoned our dead, and our own death.

For most of human history, death's imminence was close. In every city from Babylon onwards, you would have encountered the sick and dying on almost every street. You died where you lived, in the village, your home, surrounded by neighbours and family. Just as death remains visible with the poor today especially in what is called the Third World.

In the richer Western world, we have changed the public face of death by inventing better sewage drains, better drugs, training doctors and nurses, drinking cleaner water, eating a better diet and living longer.

Now though the very sight and presence of the dead has become anathema to us. When we get sick we think it is only natural to go to hospital. A lot of people do get better in hospital but a lot of other people also go to die there. Disposing of the dying and keeping their corpses out of sight has become an intrinsic central task of every Western hospital.

Inside the Western Death Machine, the dead quickly disappear into solid-sided trolleys and blank-doored mortuaries before being passed along to undertakers and then buried or burned in state-designated facilities.

We have, falsely, come to believe that the bodies of the dead are owned by the state and that myriad laws must be obeyed, and forms filled in (something to do with public health and safety, possibly contamination of the public water supply?) before you are allowed to dig a hole in the ground and put a dead human inside it. We have lost control.

Fewer and fewer people ever go see their dead or go to funerals. And so fewer and fewer people know how to hang out in mortality or with the grieving relatives. Or know what to say to the kid who has just lost his father.

Over time our social space around death has shrunk smaller and smaller until we are no longer sure how we as individuals should handle mortality. Even before the virus struck, death had become like an indecipherable language to us.

———

Why is the sight of the dead, even in a photograph, now so rare that it is easy to believe death is something that only ever happens to other people?

Other people? Yes, other people who die far, far away in another galaxy.

Like the newspapers and television stations that readily apologise over including 'distressing' pictures of starving, dying children in foreign war zones while reporting on foreign war zones where children are starving and dying. And where any images of the actual dead are pixelated because the sight of their dead flesh is deemed an offence against public decency.

The internet is filled with explicit sexual imagery but images of the dead and the dying are deemed more intensely intrusive, shocking, almost forbidden, than any orgy.

We are consumed too by an existential fear as if dying itself was infectious. A contagion. Convincing ourselves we can't visit the sick because what could we possibly talk about? Apart from their death? Even if it is just a 'mundane' cancer?

But death, dying, the whole lot, it is all still purposeless. Isn't it?

Old people, beyond their sell-by date, marooned in smelly old folks' homes, half of them demented, 'empty husks', who would be better off dead anyway.

Or those cancer victims on Facebook posts, bald women, vowing to run futile marathons or knit patch quilts as part of some breast cancer fundraising thing.

The whole lottery of our viral plague, fathoming the why and how of those who died, those who survived and

those who had it coming with some 'pre-existing condition'. Diabetes. Or obesity. Or some lung condition. The
wrong sort of genes.

What about those teenagers who overdose on heroin,
or get stabbed, or something else? It is just all far too grim
even to think about never mind get involved with. Morbid.

But if death is all so purposeless, or meaningless, does
even your own life matter too in the end?

Why are you so uniquely special? Why should anyone
else care about you?

And if your life does matter then so too do the lives,
and deaths, of others.

Dying hasn't changed at all. We have.

It is our generation who have lost the experience of
death as a wider collective social experience. Something
we have all shared and therefore something we can all talk
about freely together.

It is odd that the one thing we all share in common we
never talk about.

Something you too could personally talk about with
your friends?

Maybe? Or at least once? Why not?

We spend a huge amount of our time tweeting and
twitching, working on our feelings, dating or not dating,
or talking about what we want or what we think will
happen. But in all the white noise do you ever connect
with another human on what it feels inside to be mortal?

To be able to say a few simple words like: 'I have this fear, like what happened to my father, any cough, back pain, my mind just starts racing thinking it's the same cancer.'

'I think about the kids, what's going to happen to them without me?'

'I can't understand how I even ended up here in this shitty life.'

Not some great revelatory moment but one of those casual just-slipping-into-the-conversation sharing of thoughts in between the usual round of the weather, the complaining about your moan-face boss who drives you mad, the traffic, and the best curry takeaway.

If you feel you've never had the chance to have that conversation maybe it explains why we all feel so lonely about dying?

We are so far down the road of denial we are often confused about what real grief is.

We gather easily round for the flash-mob lighting of candles and the creation of flower shrines in our now common media funereal rite for those who die in public massacres or are pop-star famous. And we validate our feelings as if real in Facebook, Instagram posts and #StayStrong retweets.

But oddly we hardly ever go to real funerals of all the real people we know. And we never see the dead.

Of course that is a generalisation but when did you last go to a funeral? Or touch a corpse?

Childishly we have invented a nonsense vocabulary of euphemisms like 'passed' to avoid saying the Death word out loud and then attempt to censor any who challenge this make-believe orthodoxy because what right has anyone to upset the bereaved by stating a mortal truth?

We are too afraid of death.

———————

Okay.

So how should we control our fear and conquer death?

Well we could invent a whole new caste of priests, death-professionals and bereavement therapists to re-educate ourselves about death and grief and sign up for lots of Death Studies courses. Write up a few PhDs? Which is sort of what we are doing even though that is just another way of abnegating our responsibility by making death someone else's responsibility.

Or we could do something much simpler and just copy what the Irish, and our ancestors, have been doing about death for the last 25,000 years in the rite of the Wake.

Rather than run away from death we could do what we always used to do and gather as mortals, cry, feast, drink, talk, sing and stand alongside the bereaved as they bury their dead. And all face death together.

If you have never been to an Irish Wake and only seen the movie version, you probably think the Wake is just another Irish piss-up.

A few maudlin drunks in the back room of a dingy bar muttering and weeping into their pints of Guinness about their Uncle Johnny who they buried sometime earlier that day.

But you would be dead wrong.

The Wake is both the oldest rite and oldest faith of humanity, dating back to long before the fall of Troy, the raising of the pyramids in Egypt around 3000 BC and the creation of the first city Uruk on the plains of Mesopotamia in 4500 BC. Long before Yahweh, Abraham, Jesus or the Prophet appeared our Neolithic stone tool ancestors ritually mourned over their dead.

Even the peoples of the New World like the Aztecs, separated from the cultures of the Old World for over 25,000 years, used keening women to wail and grieve over the dead in the same rituals as the Egyptians, the Irish, the ancient Greeks and the Romans.

The Wake is as much a part of the human story as our DNA, and elements of the Wake underpin the funeral rites of almost every human culture. For some reason the Irish kept going with the Wake long after other northern European societies stopped waking their dead over the last two centuries.

In the Wake, our ancestors believed in something we have almost forgotten all about – the rite of burial.

Before you got to go to Heaven, Hell, or Hades your living relations, your community, had to go through a whole series of rites with your dead body to make sure you reached the afterlife. Even in death they had an obligation to look after you so your spirit would find peace. We all needed a proper wake and funeral to close mortality's wound.

For our ancestors the Wake, the funeral and all the attendant rituals were life necessities. The bodies of those we loved had to be guarded and protected in the hours and days after their death, set rituals played out and observed, and the remains burned or buried in special ceremonies.

The living and the dead remained bound together in a web of predetermined ritual and social obligation whose ultimate goal was to restore order to the natural world. Various gods and the spirit of the dead person had to be appeased by cycles of prayers, the gathering of mourners, feasting, drink, the telling of stories, and burial rituals.

Hidden away inside the Wake are countless other therapeutic mechanisms that by design or default are enacted to contain and channel the disorder of death and grief and heal the living.

A wake can be a joyous event as well as being sad. And even in the saddest of deaths, where hope is hard to conjure, a wake can still be cathartic.

A wake is a communal gathering to affirm irreparable change, the deadness of the deceased, and a public stage where potentially dangerous behaviours, uncontrolled grief, keening, the pleasures of sorrow, the bonds of shared mourning, can be acted out safely. A catharsis for the most powerful emotions we will ever experience.

A wake is an encompassing, an act of mortal solidarity within a community to overcome the rupture of an individual death and a prescribed ritual where the physicality of death, a corpse, is tamed, neutralised, and assigned a place in the order of the world. Feasting, and drink, to replenish the hungers of the mourners and entice the bereaved away from the abstinences of grief, is an intrinsic element.

A wake is also an act of affirmative compassion where the wisdom of the past and the paradigm manual of how to live and die, the rules, were transferred down the generations. A communal act of care.

And as strange as this might sound a wake is also a fertility rite, a promise of regeneration that from the lamenting wombs of those keening women, the *Mná Caointe* in Irish, newborn sons and daughters will spring to replace the fallen.

Sex and death are our oldest twin compulsions and they defiantly intermingle in the Wake in ancient games and sexualised debauchery. Nothing so provokes the hunger for sexual consummation, the need of a warm Other, than death's presence.

In some places in the world those old faiths, old beliefs, live on and the wisdom of the past is carried forward. There is an island, far out to the West, rising, sea-plucked, spray-lashed, a citadel of stone, walled deep in the blue ocean where faith in the Wake still burns bright.

I know that place because my father and mother were born there and all my ancestors too for the last seven generations, my great, great, great, great, great, great, mothers and fathers. My family have lived in the same small oceanside village on an island off the coast of Mayo in Ireland for the last 250 years, probably longer still.

This island of stone, mountain and elemental fury rocked by the wild surging Atlantic Ocean has never been an important place in the world. Nor has living there ever been easy. But the basic faith of the islanders, that mortal being incarnate in flesh shall not live, love or die alone, remains one of the oldest of humanity and the island now acts as one of the last living archives of those ancestral beliefs. When someone dies, the islanders still go in great numbers to their neighbour's house to wake through the night with the dead body. The family of the deceased are never left alone. Women will join in the keen, the cry of grief, and the tears of the bereaved.

In the following days the islanders will fill the family home sitting vigil besides the corpse in the open coffin, help make tea and sandwiches, keep the bereaved family company, and share in the grieving. There will be feasting, drink, laughter, stories told, and perhaps secrets revealed.

Men from the village will volunteer to dig a grave by hand on the nearby Slievemore mountain. The villagers will be there too, crowding the pews in the local church for the funeral Mass and on the mountain, carrying the coffin on their shoulders, at the burial and reaching out to the bereaved to shake their hands, hundreds and hundreds, to offer their sorrow at the loss.

In the same graveyard on Slievemore mountain, a forest of gravestones marks out centuries of the same repeated patterns of burial and of mourning. The oldest inscriptions on the weathered black and grey gravestones list those who died in the 1800s while a nearby shrine, a holy well set beside a now fallen ancient Celtic cross, dates from the twelfth century.

Yet even these markers are almost the youngest graves on the mountain. Higher up along what was once an ancient treeline, stretch a long line of Neolithic tombs dating from 6000 BC. Huge slabs of rocks some weighing as much as thirty tonnes have been dragged for hundreds of metres by these Neolithic people, using only stone tools and muscle power, then carefully mounted on other stone pillars to form burial chambers for their dead. Each of these tombs was in use for hundreds of years and contained the remains of many individuals. The dead mattered to these Neolithic people too.

In some form the rite of the Wake has been practised continuously on this remote Irish island for the last six thousand years.

Why did the Wake last so long? Why did our ancestors in every community across the globe repeat the same recognisably similar public funereal rituals over and over again when another human died?

What is it about the Wake that our forefathers found so valuable, so useful?

Does the Wake make it easier to conquer death or cope with grief?

What was the knowledge these ancestors passed down, generation to generation, in these ancient and eternal rites?

What have we lost? And how do we get that wisdom back again? What are the rules?

That is a lot of big questions for a small book but here, distilled from the wisdom of that ancient rite, are the Nine Rules you need to know to conquer death.

RULE ONE: BEING MORTAL
IS THE ONE THING
IN LIFE YOU DON'T
GET TO CHOOSE.

RULE ONE

How you deal with death defines the sort of human being you are.

Good. Bad. Fearful.

Some people like football and some people don't. Outside of prison or a viral lockdown you are generally free to do what you want with your Saturday afternoons. The music you listen to. The clothes you wear. The apps you download.

But death, dying and mortality are not hobbies or fashion trends. You can't be human without being mortal, a member of the universal Us. As long as you breathe you too are part of the living Us. When you stop you become one of the former Us, the dead.

There is no opt-out or neutral in-between. You don't get to choose.

So being indifferent to the mortality of others, strangers,

neighbours, friends, your family, even your enemies, is not some value-free lifestyle choice.

Denying the power of death, the value of those other lives, their humanity, the pain their relatives feel, is even worse.

Have you ever been to one of those European countries where you are just sitting around in some small village cafe way out in the countryside and a solitary church bell starts tolling? The sound of it, that clang-bang, echoing in the still air off the stones of the old buildings, reverberating across the valley in the summer heat.

Dong . . . Dong . . . Dong.

The bell keeps tolling on, and on, until you get so curious you ask one of the locals what's happening? They tell you that the bell is ringing for someone, maybe some old woman in the village, who is being buried today. That the sound of the bell is encouraging as many people as possible to show up at the church to support the dead person's family in what could be the saddest days of their lives.

To be there to affirm that the dead person was a somebody who had a place and position in this community.

And their death, the loss of them, means something to their family, the neighbours, maybe even to the village fishmonger who sold them fish or the same cafe owner whose pavement tables they sat at for hours and hours talking about the lottery numbers or the weather or whatever.

Dong . . . Dong . . . Dong.

Except the bell is not just tolling for the fishmonger either or anyone else who personally knew the dead person. Or cared about them enough to waste a few hours of their own life at some dead old woman's funeral. The bell is tolling out for everyone within earshot whether they want to listen or not.

The dong of the bell is sending out a message that one of us, one of the universal Us, the Mortal Us, is no longer alive and is being buried today and that means something.

Or should. A dead human. Not an 'empty shell'. Or a carcass. Or someone's pet dog. But a being who was loved by other human beings and whose death wounds the bereaved, causes them pain.

So it is only natural that you would want to reach out to help as you would with any stricken animal but principally by showing up and being there.

And because we have, or will, all suffer loss and grief one day, the bell is tolling too of the common bonds of joy, love, frailty, vulnerability, we all share in being human.

And if you don't recognise yourself amidst that congregation then who are you?

Dong . . . Dong . . . Dong.

That bell is tolling for you.

On the Irish island of my mothers and fathers an announcer on the local radio station reads out a roll call of the daily dead in an electronic version of the same tolling bell.

There is a bit of solemn music and then the daily 'deaths', their names and funeral arrangements, are read out over the air three times a day just after the local news.

An annunciation of who is no longer with us.

'The death has occurred of Francie Mulloy of Aughaclower, reposing in his residence. Removal at 5p.m. Friday to the Church of Our Lord the Redeemer followed by Mass of the Resurrection at 10a.m. on Saturday and internment in the local Dunacurry graveyard.'

There is a brief pause and then the next stranger's death is read out. 'The death has occurred . . .' And on and on until the toll is finished. Across the county wake-goers, like those villagers, go in great numbers to wake with their dead neighbours, attend the removal of their dead bodies, go to the church for the funeral and pray at the graveyard for the soul of the dead person.

Other local radio stations across Ireland, in between the usual weather reports and lonesome cowboy songs, run similar death notices.

Some stations even have a 95-cents-a-minute helpline, just so you can check up on those you have missed among the recently departed.

Death is louder in Ireland, more public, and it is easier to know who within your wider community has died.

Talking out loud about the dead, not being scared to mention the D-word in public is one of the reasons why the Irish do death so well.

But the Irish understanding of how to handle death is very different too. In our Western death denial we shun the sick, minimise death and recoil from the bereaved.

Those Irish villagers do the exact opposite. They reach out to embrace the dead and their families. The villagers go to those wakes and funerals because they recognise a universal mortal kinship with the dead person and the bereaved family. They don't wait to be asked or worry about intruding.

The wake-goers believe they need to be there because the bereaved, their fellow mortals, will need them. And because they are less afraid of confronting death than we are.

And if such concern for a fellow mortal is not the best of us then it is hard to think of what else could be asked of another soul. For in that act of selfless reaching out the mourner cannot but affirm to the bereaved, and the bereaved to the mourner, the commonality of all human flesh.

Do you think it's strange? The not being asked? Or the volunteering? The 'universal kinship' thing? The unbidden reaching out.

But what if the worst thing in the world happened to you?

Your mother collapsing in the street? Your boyfriend knocked off his bike? Finding out you had cancer? Your husband dying? Losing your job? Failing your exams? Being attacked in some way? Feeling the onset of a viral sickening?

Whatever it was would you not be better off with some help, other people, instead of being alone?

Humans, because they are mortal, die all the time.

Just under one percent of the entire world population each year. Even with the coronavirus.

160,000 dead people a day. 60 million a year, or thereabouts. An even spread across the planet.

Dying is happening right now in your town too, down the block, in the local hospital, maybe somewhere on the road you take to work every day: an accident, a heart attack in the local hardware store, a fall, cancer, suicide, a blood clot, a heroin overdose, a gunshot, or in a host of other mundane ways.

Now because people die at roughly the same rate everywhere across the globe, the same death bell is tolling at exactly the same rough one percent rate a year in your community too.

The bell might be tolling silently and the names not read out on the daytime news but if you listen, at church or in the funeral notices in the local paper, on Facebook, or just in conversation with a neighbour in the supermarket aisle, or in the office, you'll start hearing that bell loud and clear.

Dong . . . Dong . . . Dong.

Here is how you can do the maths on how many times the death bell tolls in your town. Take the population size, divide it by 100 and you more or less have the answer.

So if you live in a town of 10,000 people around 100 people will die each year.

If your town has 100,000 people the figure will be 1,000.

A city of a million, 10,000.

The same calculation will give you a reasonably accurate indicator of all the people who died in your town this year. And in fact the same number who died the year before and roughly the same number who will die next year as well. And the next.

So in a city like London or New York, with similar populations of 8.5 million each, 85,000 people will die this year. And the year after that.

Are you surprised at the number? Or that death is so predictable?

How many of the dead people in your town did you know?

Or knew that they were sick or dying? Or went to their funerals? Or know now that they are sick and dying and won't live long but haven't spoken to them?

Of course it's not just the dead people themselves.

Most of the one percent were part of families, worked in jobs, had friends and neighbours and a place in the world. The loss of their lives meant something to their children, their husbands, their neighbours, grandchildren and colleagues.

Each death like a stone in water rippled among the lives around them touching five, ten, sometimes hundreds of other people.

So each year around ten percent of the population are affected in some direct way by the deaths of others.

Do you really not know any of them? Those dead and their relatives. The bereaved?

Did you never feel any kind of connection to your son's school friend whose mother died of breast cancer far too young like mothers with breast cancer sometimes do?

Your dentist's father?

Or that family on the other side of the road whose teenage son took a heroin overdose and whose parents you can't even look at in the street out of fear?

The mother of someone you once worked with who has Stage 4 cancer?

Never heard that so-and-so's father in the office has died?

Or that woman in the cubicle three rows along who dropped down dead somewhere?

Or went out of your way and asked about when and where her funeral was going to take place? So you could turn up?

Or what about your own wider family connections?

The people from your past who live in other towns, maybe the other side of the country? Your aunt, that uncle who bought you your first beer, your dead father's second wife. Your college room-mate?

The list goes on. We are always more connected than we think. Did you ever think of them? Yes?

But then there is the flying all the way there. Taking time off. And the cost. Just to show up? For what? A funeral?

Maybe if you weren't so busy at work, or they had died at a more convenient time, you definitely would have gone. Or thought about it at least. Maybe next time?

Really?

But did you ever even call them, those relatives, the bereaved, your old friends?

Get in touch just to say you were sorry? Not a text or a post but a phone call? Long-distance. The sound of a human voice on the line.

Even though you know and they know it is not going to change anything? Except perhaps to make them feel less alone knowing that other people have noticed they have lost someone they love?

Maybe you knew but didn't care?

Or maybe you were afraid? Deathstruck.

About what to say. The whole awkward thing. Worrying about saying the wrong thing?

Make them more sad when sad, of course, is bad. Upset them.

Or maybe you were just afraid? Of death?

Or maybe you did hear some of the details but reckoned those dyings and deaths had nothing to do with you or your family? Old news from another country you no longer visit. Or ever need to.

I mean who wants to intrude? Cancer, dementia, adult nappies, an overdose, all that stuff is private. Shameful.

Can you even imagine what it must be like when your kid, your brother, commits suicide?

Devastating. Those parents, anyone, will just want to be left alone, to get on with their grief in private and not be bothered. Won't they? So it doesn't really matter anyway about you not calling. Thank goodness.

And anyway if people want to talk about those sorts of things then they will. It's up to them. Grief counsellors and all that stuff. Professionals.

The whole thing, dying, death, is just so embarrassing, isn't it?

It's hard enough even to look at the parents when you see them out, after knowing what happened. Wondering what they are going through.

What can you say?

But here is another question – have you ever thought about asking?

Yes, asking them if they don't want to talk about it?

People are a mystery. Maybe they really do want to talk but just don't know if other people will listen? When you get to share your grief it's usually a relief.

You talk and talk saying the same things over and over, to different people, repeating the same stories, feeling the same sad things, tearing up and crying. But the more and more you talk, the more you cry, little by little the sadness slowly leaches away because you are healing yourself just by talking out loud. A catharsis of emotion that gradually diminishes the terrible loneliness, anger and isolation of grief.

The 'why fucking me?' that rips inside at your heart.

Saying it out loud, sharing those inside thoughts, is like a release even if it's just the same words being said over and over again. Sometimes for years, decades.

'You know I hate watching the Cup Final because it always reminds me of when I used to watch it with my dad.'

'I don't eat lasagne now – can't. It was her favourite.'

'I listen to her voicemails on my phone, over and over. I can't wipe them.'

'Why did he have to die? Why?'

'I would kill them all if I could. All of her friends who did nothing to help her that night. Why didn't they do something when they saw what she was like. Call an ambulance?'

'She should have said something, told us she wasn't coping. I would have been up there like a shot. Getting her a doctor. Why did she do that to herself?'

'I'll never help her buy a wedding dress, never hold my grandchildren in my arms.'

'Our lives are changed forever and he is walking around like nothing ever happened, laughing at us. My darling boy is gone. That scumbag murderer.'

Leaving people 'to grieve in private' is like leaving someone imprisoned in the worst dungeon cell in the world hoping that after three years in solitary they will feel better. They won't.

So just maybe you could ask them if they would like to talk anyway?

How hard could it be to walk over the road to that family whose son or daughter died of an overdose, or killed themselves, and say you were sorry about the loss of their child. And maybe ask if there was anything you could do to help.

However hard and embarrassing that walk could be, even if you are rejected, it still won't be a hundredth of the pain they are suffering 'in private' from being unable to share the agony of their grief beyond themselves.

What about if you didn't have to walk across the road alone to ask the family because there had already been a public event where their community had all turned up to support them?

Just turned up without being asked or invited because it was a social obligation to recognise the loss and pain and show respect for their dead? Because it was the right thing to do?

An event where the dead kid's parents howled with grief and rage into the world and other people wept alongside them in a great outpouring of emotion? And then helped bury their son or daughter with all the dignity they could muster on that sad day.

So it was all a bit clearer what those parents were feeling and what sort of help you could offer?

Would that sort of event, an Irish Wake, or something like it, not just be a better way to deal with death in the first place?

In your head when the funeral bell tolls, even silently, does it always toll for someone else, remote and entire?

Or when you hear the bell does it, in the words of the English poet John Donne, toll for thee?

We don't have a choice about being mortal but we do have a choice about what sort of mortals we want to be.

Good. Bad. Fearful.

How we react personally to the sound of that bell, the pain of Others, defines how human we are because it also defines our attitudes to the greater Us, the sick, the bereaved, our community, society and ultimately our own personal anxiety about dying.

Your fear of death. And your ability to love someone other than yourself.

The choice is always yours.

Do you reach out to embrace your own mortality or recoil away in fear?

Do you recognise yourself in the Us?

Do you want to be human?

RULE TWO: IF WE DID
NOT DIE LIFE WOULD
BE TERRIBLE.

RULE TWO

Supposing we stopped dying and got to live forever? Not just you or me but every one of the Us. Wouldn't it be great?

Think of all the pain, those cancer deaths, malaria, dementia, the coronavirus, all that suffering, grief, loss, that would never happen. The lives saved.

This is not my original idea.

Becoming a god or getting to be an angel in Heaven and living forever is a common enough theme in most of the world's religions. Billions of people are praying for immortality to happen to them every day even though they believe they will have to die first.

Nor is the hunger for eternal life restricted to the religious.

There is a new set of prophets on the planet called anti-death evangelists, biohackers who say that immortality is almost somewhere within our grasp if we can only snip off the right bit of DNA code. Swallow the right combination of so-called vitamin pills. Re-engineer our telomeres. Bend our double helix to an immortal will.

Somewhere already in a Silicon Valley laboratory, bio-gerontologist researchers, with billions of dollars raised in venture capital behind them, are working on a gene editing plan to extend the lifespans of their masters-of-the-universe backers who are too important to die along with the rest of us and plan to extend their lifespan by fifty, a hundred years. Why not a thousand?

Their new plan, actually just another version of an old plan, is to conquer death by not dying.

Alchemy.

But what would happen back on Earth if an immortality plan were ever implemented for real and we changed the human existential code from begotten, born and die to something with infinity in it?

What would our Brave New Immortal World be like?

Begotten, born and die. Three words. As a formula it doesn't sound like the underpinning of all human perception, thought and knowledge but when you intellectually unpack the box lots of very big human existential concepts pop out: Causality, Time, Order, Language, Thought.

Let's start with Time.

On a normal mortal day you get up, eat breakfast, and go to school to pass your exams so you can study at college or university. Or you go to work so you can pay your bills or save enough money to go on holiday to reward yourself. Or maybe you are lucky and like your job and are hoping to get promoted soon. Or you are working your way towards a wonderful retirement.

We spend a lot of our present life planning on becoming something in the future: a teacher, a doctor, a mother, a counsellor, a footballer or someone famous.

Usually we want to become something because we think it will make us happier, more fulfilled. 'By the time I am twenty-five I want to be a millionaire,' sort of thing. Earn enough to put down a deposit on a house. Or we want to get that PhD, run that marathon, climb Kilimanjaro, lose our belly fat, to somehow be a better person. Retire at sixty with lots of cash.

As we age we all spend time either berating or forgiving ourselves for what we have and have not done in life because we are *only* in our twenties, or thirties, or forties, fifties, or sixties or seventies. And because far, far away in the distance we all know our time, and being, runs out.

No one lives forever. Or not yet.

But why would you get out of bed in the morning to become anything if the future, the whole getting-older future, disappeared into infinity because you were never going to die?

What would 'the things you had to do today' be if the future stretched limitless before you? Why not wait

49

until the next century? Why would you bother to develop any skills at all if you could never die? Or ever go for a jog?

I find it difficult to grasp what a human infinity would feel like. But supposing we thought of it like being sent into deep space in some rocket ship to the far end of the galaxy and the journey was going to take millions and millions of years to some distant star. And then some. So it would be impossible to foresee when the journey would end.

On my spaceship what would be the point of me organising a diary for 2023 or 2033 or 20333 when even the notion of a year, 365 days, is utterly trivial?

Would you organise a diary for a blink of your eye?

Our understanding of becoming anything, a mother, an astronaut, a doctor, or a waiter, would evaporate.

Life is a mortal calculus.

I choose to study engineering at university for three years because I think I am good at maths and engineering will be a rewarding career. Or I apply to be a nurse because I want to work in medicine. Or I train every day to become a professional footballer because I am good at kicking balls around and want to be rich and famous and support my family.

And I don't have an infinite number of choices to make.

But what does it mean if I decide to study engineering for three hundred years? Or stay at university for three thousand years until I have qualified in every single one of the hundreds of degree courses available?

Or train for the Premier Immortal League and play on the 11-man England football squad forever. Or maybe, to give someone else a chance, just for ten thousand years?

But why should I train to 'become' anything when in theory I could be everything? Or nothing? Why would anything matter?

Our becoming something or someone, our identity, our Being, is dependent on the limitations of time, not its elasticity.

We live in Change. In Finitude. All around us, winter summer, spring, autumn, nature blossoms, falls, decays. Instinctively, we too measure time in human lifespans.

We grow up, become an adult, age, grow older, grow grey.

But in our Brave New Immortal World this existential understanding of linear time would collapse. The concept of 'tomorrow' or 'the day after', a 'decade', or 'a century' would be meaningless. We would lose all measure of future and past and live in an eerie eternal present Indefinite. But what would such an eternal Indefinite be like?

Would our bodies stop ageing? Would we be frozen in our particular age at the moment of immortal declaration? So if you are two when the immortal bell tolls you are forever two and thirty-six if you are thirty-six? Or ninety-six?

But how much fun could it be to be forever two? Or thirty-six? Or be forever demented if you happened to be demented when you were made eternal?

Will each individual cell in our body be immortalised at our eternal genesis, neither decaying nor being replaced? Or if you have arthritic knees and a dodgy heart will we get to magically hit the Restore button to a former time when your body was young and alter linear Time as well? Remake the past?

Could you ever become pregnant, give birth and have a child in such a world of stasis? Or would 'potential' mother and foetus be locked together *in utero* forever?

In the mortal world we are begotten when a swimming sperm fertilises an egg. The egg becomes an embryo, which becomes a foetus, and a baby.

Being begotten is a causal process running through cellular division, chronological time and ruled by the laws of physics and biology. The same process that delivers a birth, a growing child and joy, hope, renewal and change, happens because the future is open and at risk. Without proper food, care, vaccinations, love, the child will die. And in time the same laws of physics and causality will also determine that child's individual biological death.

But can causality exist within an Indefinite Universe? Can you be a 'mother' forever? A child who never ages? Never dies?

Outside this book I am the father of three children. My fatherhood only makes sense if my children grow up and they potentially become fathers and mothers themselves and that one day I die too like all the mothers and fathers before me. Could I really 'father' my children forever? How can they ever become adults unless they cease to be children? If they don't grow up, age, who am I? And who are they?

What about another immortal scenario where you can grow up, become, but once you get to be an adult you live forever? The Hollywood version of immortality. Eternal Happy Families.

So that means some bits of the immortal universe are ruled by something we might vaguely recognise as the normal rules of causality and some bits are not.

Sometimes the apple falls downward from the tree and sometimes it doesn't. Cells divide and then they don't. Which really means that even this version of our projected immortal world is again nothing like our world and our human understanding at all.

Trying to imagine a universe where humans beings get to live forever is like trying to imagine a universe where none of the laws of physics apply. And language and thought spiral into nonsense.

A river where the waters never flow. A rain that never falls but stays immobile in the air. An Earth that never spins.

If we are immortal do we breathe? Would we still get hungry? Do we get to eat meat, which means killing other things that clearly then don't share in our eternal life? If we don't need to eat do we then need sleep? Would we ever get tired?

And if we did get hungry but didn't eat what would happen then if we still can't die? And if you don't need to eat to survive what would hunger, or sexual desire, be like?

The same questions could go on and on whirling away into further nonsense.

To make eternal life work we would have to jettison the laws of physics and causality that order and determine human perception, thought and language. And love.

You can only love someone or something because you care about what happens to them and that something bad, death, destruction, could possibly happen to endanger that love. And also because you hope, if you love another human, that they will care about you too.

But nothing can ever happen to an eternal being because they are eternal. Nor by their nature could they ever love anything because that would mean loving something that wasn't eternal.

Instead of the universe being ordered and predictable our immortal universe would be chaotic, disordered and unpredictable. You would not be free to live forever but condemned to live forever.

The heaven of immortality would be hell on Earth and

that is before we even get to the big question of what is the point of being immortal anyway?

Or of living to be 150, 200?

To live longer?

Yes but what is the purpose of just living longer? Think hard about the answer.

Would you share your new longer life with those you love? Or just watch them all die out around you?

What about if the real plan was just for a few rich people, Billionaire Gods, who could pay the bio-gerontologists millions of dollars each, to get to live a lot longer at least? Maybe two hundred years?

But is this smaller warp in causality, their failure to change, to age and die, any more physically conceivable? How could such an entity co-exist within a causal world? How do you make yourself immune from the laws of physics?

Supposing our Billionaire Gods decided to forgo all exercise and gorge themselves safe in the knowledge that their body's dividing cells were now semi-immortal. Would they become obese? And if they did would they still be immune from a heart attack at 40 stone? Would their kneecaps never give out even if they jogged eternally between the Earth and Jupiter? Or their skin cells be free of the risk of cancerous mutation from spending their extra 100,000 hours suntanning on the beach?

Even when we think abstractly the neurons in our

brains are firing up in a causal chain that alters, minutely, our brain chemistry and physically alters the world at least inside our head. Tiny changes that in time alter us, alter our brain chemistry.

Although we don't know why one in three of every 85-year-olds has Alzheimer's, that is itself a result of processes of change within the brain.

So how can you even think and not change the world? And if you do make changes how do you stay the same? You can't.

Like the mortal, these semi-immortals don't get to choose which bits of causality apply and which bits don't. Before they get to conquer death the bio-gerontologists will have to conquer time, physics and the universe. And philosophy.

All these immortal thought possibilities might seem a bit childish until you get to the fatal simple truth about what they uncover about our immortal fantasies.

Our mortality is not just coded into our DNA but also into our thought, language and our perception of time, the universe and the purpose of our lives.

Descartes the philosopher said: I think, therefore I am. But ordinary mortals operate under a different aphorism: I die, therefore I am.

Even in thought we cannot escape our nature. Everything that we love, aspire to, think of, even dream about is bound by our mortality.

Embedded in the Wake, in the wisdom of our ancestors, is the same mortal logic made flesh – we are because we are finite – and here in the touch of a corpse is visceral proof of this living truth.

The world makes sense to us because we die, not because we don't.

RULE THREE: PRETENDING YOU ARE IMMORTAL IS A BAD IDEA.

RULE THREE

Apart from the suicidal, no one wants to die.

But just because we conceptually know we will die doesn't mean we ever stop trying to deny the certainty of our death. Our capacity for immortal self-deception is relentless.

For sure everyone else dies but when we think about our own personal future we swim in an ocean of time that forever recedes ahead into infinite possibility.

A personal exception for ourselves as the deathless Special Case.

A unique anomaly to the general mortal rule – Me.

Special Case?

That's a silly idea. What sort of idiot could ever think like that?

Here is a simple immediate test you can do to detect Special Case thinking.

Just take your birth year, add the average life expectancy for your sex and country and work out the answer.

If you are reading this book in the Western world adding 80 onto your birth year will give you a reasonably accurate forecast of your likely life expectancy. A good enough statistical guess for working out when you are really going to die.

So for example if you were born in 1990 + 80 years equals 2070.

Your Death Date. Roughly.

So why don't you try writing down your own Death Date here now?

Your birth year + 80 equals _____.

Yes here on this page.

Right now.

_____.

I know we could get into lots of arguments as to why the same arithmetic won't apply in your particular case and maybe you'll live a decade longer – your grandparents all lived into their nineties – but those actuarial tables, based on the aggregates of millions of birth and death statistics, are usually lethally accurate.

Do you not believe me?

Or you don't like gimmicks in books?

Or you think the question is some stupid trick? Or rude?

What about writing the date down on a separate piece of paper?

Or are you worried that by writing your Death Date down it will be bad luck?

So if you do write the date down you'll then die sooner?

Or maybe you just don't want to think about your Death Date because you know somehow that you're going to live a lot longer, being a Special Case?

Or you just don't want to think about your death?

Or maybe you just don't want to die?

———

Why is it so hard writing it down or even thinking about it?

Even though by now the number is inside your head anyway? 2025, 2037, 2049, 2061, 2087. Two thousand and something. Four numbers on a page.

It's not like it is a death sentence, just a statistical number, a probability.

Would your actuarial Death Date be easier if you said it out loud?

Why don't you? Because now you know the secret anyway?

Of course you could live well into your late eighties, beat the odds, even make it into your nineties.

Your birth year + 90 equals _____? Does that make you feel better? The writing-in easier?

But are you seriously going to beat the odds on making it to a hundred, become a centenarian, when only one in 29,000 men will ever do so?

Numbers like 1:29,000 can be hard to imagine but supposing we thought about them like some massive Russian roulette-style revolver packed with 28,999 bullets and one empty chamber. And then you spun the barrel and put the gun to your head hoping when you pulled the trigger that you'd chance on that one blank chamber.

Surely no one sane would ever take the risk, unless of course you thought you really were a Special Case?

Now if you are female the odds drop sharply in your favour and one woman in 5,000 will now make it through the 100-year turnstile. But even at those odds would you ever take the shot on a revolver loaded with 4,999 bullets?

And all this Death Date stuff doesn't include all the other health provisos we need to get clear, dementia, arthritic knees, leaky heart valves and a host of other degenerative diseases of old age you'll need to negotiate before you qualify to be able to read your 100-year birthday telegram from Buckingham Palace or the letter from the White House.

Odds work both ways, remember.

What if your personal End Date Number was one of those pulled out of the great genetic lottery for cancer at thirty-seven just to give the other players their statistical chance of making it to 100? Or eighty?

Aren't we just playing with statistics?

Empty numbers that don't say anything useful about your life or your death?

Yes and no. The exact date of your death is unpredictable. But what is interesting is our aversion to recognising that our death, our lifespan, is very predictable. Certain.

That there is a terminal date on our individual existence tied up with our generation, our birth decade. An exactitude that cannot be negotiated away. Not the theoretical sometime-in-the-future endless possibility of being a Special Case.

As it turns out this little exercise of trying to get you to write down your Death Date, and failing or succeeding, is not just a gimmick in a book.

Putting down the figure on paper is a small first step in consciously accepting the mortal limitations of your own life. The brightness of knowledge and acceptance against the fuzzy deceit of denial.

A little act of mortal courage.

So here's mine. I know I will never see Halley's Comet again, due back in the night sky in 2062. I will be dead when the comet returns.

I saw the comet in 1986 when I was living in Namibia, in southern Africa, and was twenty-seven years old. A bright pencil of light that for a non-astronomer made the night sky three-dimensional. I went out with friends into the desert and lay on my back and stared up at this strange streak of light among the infinite stars of the southern skies for the first and what will be my last time.

I was born in 1959 and that means, if I am lucky, I will die in the 2040s in my eighties, two decades before the comet is seen again. And the world will go on without me.

Theoretically, if I lived to be 103, I might just be able to stare up into the night sky and see the return of this celestial visitor. An old man who has escaped the bounds of time. But that is just a vain imagination of my own mind. More Special Case denial.

I will be long dead by the 2050s, as will most of my generation. As sure a bet as the sun rising in the east every morning. And that too is okay because I am already lucky to still be here in the 2020s.

If you did manage to write the date down then do award yourself a gold mortal star.

If you didn't this time there is always tomorrow.

And maybe you will get to see Halley's Comet as I never will.

But here is one last odd question.

Isn't it strange this is the first time you've ever even thought about it?

Not the comet but your Death Date?

Do you want to try again? _____

———————

As a Special Case, even when confronted by a terminal diagnosis, we often operate a peculiar Get-Out-of-Death magical thinking syndrome that exempts us from the general universal fate.

We are collective suckers for every medical guru, pharmaceutical company, Wizard of Oz vitamin pill salesman, 'organic' nutritionist or oncologist wearing a white coat touting the latest 'miracle' cure.

We want to believe in the magical dust they sell. The fables they offer. Those con men from California, the bio-gerontologists, and their newfound religion of slimy green juice and pill-popping salvation.

Or the specialist disciples of such and such a prestigious medical school with their arrow case of degrees, magic bullets, latest experimental drug trial, white coats and an intent bedside manner.

We really do.

Slash, poison, burn too even when it hurts. The miracle feed, the new immunotherapy elixir, from some big-name pharmaceutical company, dripped through your veins at US$12,000 a shot that will, when all else has failed, reverse the cellular division of cancerous mitosis and personally save our skin when every other quitter just dies.

Blinding ourselves in eager belief that we can somehow negotiate with our own biological finitude, our mortal essence. A real-life game of pressing that Russian roulette revolver up against your skull and wilfully pulling the trigger.

The cruel delusion too that some secret herbal formula touted by other self-qualified charlatans can rework the balance. The super ingredients, the alpha omega vitamin juicer pack, the magic diet, that will kill our cancer, rejuvenate our skin, hair, breasts, penis, boost our immune system, stave off mortality and provide the answer to our foolish prayers.

Sadder yet is that vain falsehood that through some past athletic, financial or moral worthiness we shall prove ourselves to be a 'fighter', and so personally stand up to cancer, beat this disease, win the war and be spared the fate of the common herd.

In the end all the 'fighters' die just like 'losers', for the inescapable reason that fighters are mortal too.

Maybe it is one of our great human strengths and our weakness – the ability to deceive ourselves. A Special Case.

It might seem old-fashioned, even banal, but the best antidote yet invented for such magical self-delusional thinking is an old-fashioned Irish Wake. Or some other ritual like it. There right in front you, open in the coffin, chillingly cold to the touch, is the fleshy corpse proof that there is no real Special Case exemption in the known universe and that your indefinite future is going to end somewhere. The human metre clock of existence.

And that one day the dead person in the box is going to be you.

Actually there is one other trick we often pull to reassert our personal immunity from death – we blame the corpse.

How many did she smoke a day?

What did she expect?

They must have had a 'pre-existing condition'.

Look at the weight on him. Fat fuck. Never did an hour's exercise in his life. Or looked after himself.

I get myself checked every year. The full medical.

Always stuffing her face.

Yep even the colonoscopy.

Sad, the poor. They die young.

Drink, drugs.

It's all in the genes. My grandmother was ninety-three.

I ran a marathon last weekend.

They know they're killing themselves but they won't stop. Will they?

He must have done something to himself, you know, to get that kind of cancer?

Disassociation.

The 'Them' and the 'They'.

We use those terms a lot when we want to distance ourselves, the my Me, or the our Us, from another invented class of humans who we want to separate from, or despise, or want to subjugate or enslave. 'They' are not like 'Us' and so deserve their lesser fate, the chains, the poverty, even their death.

And that we are personally a Special Case, an exception.

We so build mental walls to create Otherness.

We watch the TV news and see the same atrocities over and over again: murders, missing girls, terrorist massacres, school shooters, earthquakes, floods, famines and plagues. Then we switch off, go to work the next day and get on with the rest of our lives.

Mostly, the danger never reaches us, never touches our lives because thankfully all these bad things are usually happening somewhere else to other people in another country on the far side of the world. Or at least a few hundred miles away. You can turn the TV off and it's like everything you've just seen never happened. It's easy not to care.

Or pay much attention because it will never happen to you – until it does and death in whatever fashion, viral or not, comes knocking on your door and shatters your life.

Most of the time, because of that one percent rule, death comes dressed in the rags of everyday casualty.

In another life when I worked as a reporter, I watched the daily dead of a Western city, perfect strangers, come to be disembowelled, sawn, sampled and sewn up in the investigation of the causes of their demise. The happenstance ending of so many ordinary lives.

Inside Hades' fortress, the city mortuary, there were sluices and tiles, bodies on the slab and the living dressed up in gowns and yellow wellington boots getting on with the cutting.

Yesterday, or the day before, these dead had been somebodies: grandmothers, dads, postmen, drug addicts, lovers and retired teachers. They had friends, families, workmates, jobs, houses, savings, holiday plans, bills to pay and dogs to be walked.

Their endings coincided mostly with quiet fallings-off: found dead in their apartments, accidents, collapses and overdoses. Then ambulances and CPR and sirens blaring, police calls, bedside vigils, tears, shock; the raw edge of all existence, its mundane descent into nothingness and the bureaucratic prescription of the Western Death Machine.

Outside the building, somewhere, spread across the city in brick streets, bungalows, and in tower blocks there was still a river of fresh grief and pain, daughters, children and husbands weeping, wounded in the loss, trailing back to each of these muted casualties.

But here in the morgue's fluorescent calm all that was over now. These gathered dead, naked, cold and flaccid, with their smudged-out tattoos of roses and skulls on hips and forearms, were no more than diagnoses: heart attacks, strokes, mesothelioma, cancers, suicides. And opiate highs gone wrong.

The ordinary dead.

I got friendly with one of the pathologists, who drove too fast and liked to drink, and asked him if he could ever imagine being one of his clients, here for the cutting.

'Only once,' he said, though he had post-mortemed the bodies of thousands, upon thousands, of former people.

His nemesis had been a railway crash, statistically as rare as being struck dead by lightning, on a regular commuter train. An early morning train he sometimes took himself. Or another train like it. Accidents that never happen.

Most of the dead had been in the First Class restaurant car eating breakfast, bacon and eggs, when catastrophe struck. A complex chain of the wrong bits of metal being in the wrong place as the speeding mass and momentum of two now colliding trains smashed into each other. Not that it matters now. Or then.

There is not much you can do to protect yourself when the metal tube you are travelling in comes off the rails at 140 miles an hour, through no fault of your own, and your fleshy body is smashed and torn in the debris.

A lot of the victims were middle-aged men, executives of a sort, like the pathologist.

On their way to meetings in suits, with briefcases and agendas, and paunches and pensions, and return tickets to be back home that night for a wife and two teenage children. The second car parked early at the station ready for the return drive to a green suburb somewhere, looking forward to a roast chicken dinner and a bottle of wine after the long day. With no thought of dying as part of the plan.

Day commuters who never made it home but diverted ended up battered and naked in the morgue under his knife and care. A pathologist's job is to cut dead people up and investigate why they died. You don't want them to be sad, just professional. That pathologist needed the armour of disassociation to do his job and cope with the overload of daily wreckage, failure and loss that trundled across the slab. And the reasons why he could never be Them.

Just once though, in the savage cruelty, the blindness of a train crash, of fate, his armour was pierced and he saw in their soft middle-aged, fleshy middle-class ordinariness the mirror of his own potential death. 'They were just passengers on a train eating breakfast,' he said, as if to explain.

Disassociation too is just another way of deceiving ourselves. That Us and that Them. Our own personal immortality myth. The exception to those Others.

Maybe that is why our ancestors kept on with the Wake, again and again, one mortality inoculation after another. It is a lot harder to build that wall of Otherness when it is your own father, mother or child dead before you.

Your personal dead.

People you have known all your life who succumb for no other reason than their mortality.

What was the biological crime your 47-year-old husband perpetrated against himself to deserve to die of pancreatic cancer? Or those reckless drug binges that your 62-year-old grandmother never did? Or that poor boy, a teenage child, a nephew, who fell into despair and took his own life for no real good reason since his perceived unhappiness was not so very different from the lot of other teenagers? And besides he never really meant to kill himself at all but was too young to see the lethality in his real plan of attracting some attention?

The dead being dead lose all further power of illusion and deceit. Their Otherness from Us is in their deadness and not in our fabrications of we why are nothing like them. Marathon runners, the rich and famous, the strong, the thin and the healthy, the blessed, all die too.

If we strip ourselves of our own illusions by repeated contact, the gift of being in their dead presence, then we free ourselves too of our mortal dishonesty.

The dead are both guide and teacher, in their failures, successes and transience, of what it is to be truly human.

The words on this page don't really do justice to the existential revelation of it all.

However much in your daily life you want to believe you'll live forever, your talent for self-deception will crumple in the dead's visible presence at the Wake. And if it doesn't you are in need of psychiatric help.

Our ancestors revered their dead for many reasons, some of which we no longer share, but some of which we will not escape however much we wish to deny them.

In the ancient Greek poem *The Iliad* the Trojan king Priam calls out in anguish for 'the heart-comforting embrace of my dead son in my arms' and risks his own life to retrieve Hector's body from their Greek enemies.

Priam's love for his son transcends the boundaries of life. His last act of love for his son is to bring him home to Troy for a proper burial and lay Hector to eternal rest.

Hector's death is a portent of catastrophe for the Trojans. Soon their city will fall, the men put to the sword and the women and children raped or enslaved.

Yet the last verses of Homer's great war poem, written in 700 BCE, are filled with poetic laments of Hector's loss by the Trojan women and lyrical descriptions of the elegiac wonder and splendour of his wake and funeral.

Homer's homily is straightforward; even in sadness and defeat we are at our best, our greatest, when we have the courage to conquer death by embracing our fate.

Our ancestors left us a constant message in the Wake, in the repeated corpse-encountering, a reminder against our delusions.

There is no escape from our nature.

To be human is to be mortal.

RULE FOUR: NOTHING MUCH CHANGES UNDER THE MORTAL SUN.

RULE FOUR

We are begotten, born and die under the same sun; dying in each other's lives and living on in each other's deaths.

Each one of us is born anew and, intoxicated by the shiny novelty of our becoming, the dazzle of our own generation, can foolishly believe this world has begun again and life a river that always flows forward in one linear direction in chronological time.

That the past, the emptied stone ruins, those long-dead strangers, Caesars and slaves, their half-forgotten rituals, their struggles and fears, lie as worthlessly behind us as early Pac-Man computer games, beta tape, manual type-writers and horse-drawn carts.

That we are so much cleverer, so different, so much more powerful, freer, richer and wiser, than all who have gone before and have surpassed them all. And our Brave

New World of data, internet, fabulous wealth, global communication, even our plague, has changed the universe forever.

But generational time, the lives of the many, is more like a tide flowing in and flowing out over an underlying landscape that only imperceptibly alters with each passing generation.

The rules of engagement, of what it is like to be human, hardly ever change at all.

Nothing much changes under the mortal sun.

A wall falls, old gods die and a new empire rises in the East. Or in the West.

Glittering technologies come and go.

A so-called prophet arises, filled with an old rage, offers up his version of salvation, the promise always of a brighter future despite the sacrifices and cruelties, but is in time overthrown.

A distant worthless border province falls to a barbarian horde and legions are dispatched to quell the rebellion, preserve the empire from stated ruin by the sacrifice of its soldiers, and prolong failure.

Or we set out to conquer other lands, enslave peoples, mountains, markets, at whatever cost in others' blood and treasure, even our own, for no discernible reason apart from our own aggrandisement.

The dream of an easy victory, wealth, glory, power and command, blinds those who rule to the blood price the poor, the conscripted, the credulous, will pay for their adventurous folly.

The people, at first enthusiastic, in time grow weary of higher taxes, foreign wars, the unvanquished enemy, the litany of homeward-bound dead sons, and turn against the present king.

Merchants, their eyes once bright with greed for gold, retreat in fear on the road. No one knows why.

The planet boils in drought. Or freezes. The river bursts its banks and the flood carries all before it.

The finger of God's wrath or some other fault of ours is seen in hurricanes, earthquakes and the movement of the stars.

A new version of an old religion is reborn and war waged against the heretics of the past.

Those you once trusted like a sister betray you to the enemy.

We condemn slavery but fool ourselves as to how we profit from the same whip in our own lives regardless of the price paid by others. The sugar in our tea. The cloth on our backs. The phone in our pockets. Those dying strangers at the supermarket till.

The rich prosper and the poor die or endure. Because after all there is no alternative.

Plagues sweep the Earth, rains fail, harvests wither, famine looms. The hunt for the sorcerer behind our calamity begins.

The people panic. Suddenly the mob is at the gate, looters on the prowl, and there is blood in the streets.

Chaos has come again.

The cycle returns again and again on itself. We are blind to how much our seeming newness is a re-enactment of what has gone before. Another version of the same song of our multitude.

There is joy too. As individuals we fall in love, create, build, bear children, change, and believe in the possibility of hope. We want, we long, we fail and succeed, yet remain unfulfilled.

We repeat ourselves in our hungers, hubris, addiction, sacrifice, anger, anxiety, self-destruction – the recurring patterns of our lives – more often than we think.

We fill up our minds with the white noise of fads, possessions, the blur of celebrity, the recurring flick and screen of our phones to distract ourselves from the rattling emptiness we fear.

We grow richer, more powerful, more technological but feel we are further than ever from Heaven.

We play out ready-made scripts of victimhood to explain our self-centredness to the world and absolve ourselves of any personal blame.

We say we are greater yet we suffer more, somehow, than any generation before us.

Do we ever change at all?

Or are we the same mortal restless creatures riven by

the same conflicting desires and fears as the faces that stare out from the Fayum grave mummy portraits of ancient Egypt, those individual common dead, painted nearly two thousand years ago?

One thing is certain. Our individual struggle to find meaning and happiness, and reconcile ourselves with death is forever constant.

In this seeming newness we are blinded to the power of reasoned faith and familiar ritual to guide and protect us through the predictable turning points of every life; the pathway of a child to adult to old age, the rupture of sudden death, our grief, and our forever-pending mortality.

———

When my father Sonny lay dying on the island of my ancestors and was close to the moment of death, a small group of watchers, mainly women, keeners, gathered at the foot of his bedside and sang out a Catholic prayer, the 'Five Sorrowful Mysteries of the Rosary'.

'Hail Mary full of grace, the Lord is with thee. Blessed art thou among women and blessed is the fruit of thy womb, Jesus.'

For Irish Catholics, the rosary is a familiar prayer learned in childhood. Everyone knows the words and the second verse is sung out in unison like a chorus.

'Holy Mary, Mother of God, pray for us sinners now, and at the hour of our death.'

In the small room the sound of combined voices was overwhelming. The women were calling out to this dying man, cradling him in a soothing lullaby like a child, familiar prayers, familiar sounds, into death. An act of grace that forever bound the dying man and the watchers together in that moment.

For the watchers, the singing out too was a protective mantra-like ritual performed thoughtlessly as a means of controlling their fear and excitement at being so close to death. United now together in song, death could be faced together without risk. Verse after verse, prayer after prayer.

A death prayer, a common feature in many of the world's religions, is at once a blessing, a prop and a passing on of sacred knowledge regardless of your belief in an afterlife. An epiphany. Each of these singers would pass through this experience, become armed by this knowledge, and then re-enact the same controlling calming ritual in other deaths to come.

'. . . pray for us sinners now, and at the hour of **my** death.'

My father's death lullaby was far from unique. As with the public spectacle of his death. The gathering round of family and neighbour and the saying of the rosary at the deathbed is a common feature of the Irish way of death, part of an intricate web of obligation and ritual between the living, the dying and the dead that spans many ancient cultures.

Death is louder, more open in Ireland and the network of social obligation to be there at the moment of death is deeper and more compelling. When the death call comes huge efforts in time, distance, even from the far side of the world, and cost, are made to be present in time to say goodbye to the dying or attend their Wake or funeral.

Death for the Irish, not just for a parent or close family relative, is an altogether more serious social business. Hundreds of people will come to offer their condolences to the bereaved.

In the past such obligations to the dead could transcend the loyalties of the living.

In the ancient Greek dramatist Sophocles' play *Antigone*, written in 441 BCE, the Theban princess is condemned to death for her insistence on burying her rebellious brother Polynices against the orders of King Creon – who has vengefully decreed Polynices be denied proper burial as a further punishment for his treachery.

Antigone anoints her dead brother where he lies on the battlefield with sacred oils, prays over him and covers his body with earth in a makeshift grave. Antigone chooses to obey what she and most of her ancient Greek audience would have seen as a higher divine law – the rite of burial of the dead – defies the state and so forfeits her own life.

Antigone's actions are founded in our once-universal belief system that without the proper funereal rituals your beloved dead would never pass through the perils of the afterlife and reach eternal peace. A lost soul like Polynices would roam the Earth as a dangerous restless troubled spirit and return to haunt the living.

Even in our Western death denial we retain a vestige of the same horror of irresolution.

We bring the bodies of warriors, our dead heroes like Polynices, home from the battlefield for burial in sacred ground. We hunt the waters for the bodies of those lost at sea. We condemn in horror war criminals, and murderers, who bury their victims without ritual in unmarked graves, for their inhumanity. We are repulsed by the desecration of the dead.

The memory of our ancient beliefs, a fault line into the past, lingers.

For our foremothers and fathers the unquiet dead, the unburied dead, were dangerous.

The boundaries of the supernatural and natural world could be easily broken and the spirits of the dead rise again in dreams, curses and deeds to haunt and sabotage the lives of the living: poor rains, plagues, stillborn children, hexes, new enemies upon the plain and the fall of kings.

The potential malevolence of the watching dead had to be neutralised away by the proper funereal rites and the spirit of the dead person safely banished forever below the Earth and the world's order restored.

For tens of thousands of years when death came the living stopped, gathered together, paid homage to the body of the dead person, keened, mourned, openly wept, feasted and then buried the body so they could selfishly get on with the rest of their lives.

The Wake was an act of mortal solidarity and an act of collective self-interest.

And then after 25,000 years, around the 1950s in Europe and the United States, we stopped enacting the rite of the Wake. The dead became useless, valueless. We banished ourselves from the sight and touch of a corpse. Fewer and fewer people went to funerals and death became a whisper in the Western world. Except of course among the Irish and many parts of the world beyond.

Why the Irish kept on with the Wake when such open funereal traditions died away in the rest of Europe and the United States is a puzzle but remains an indisputable cultural marker. Far from prohibiting the sight of the dead, having an open coffin for the viewing of the remains is an expected Irish social norm. Why would you not have an open coffin for your grandfather at his Wake?

In our Western Death Machine we've stopped seeing or waking our dead, but our restless invisible dead still linger with us. Denied the psychological comfort of seeing with our own eyes our dead safely buried away alongside our ancestors, the irresolution gnaws at us. The black hole of grief grows within us rather than diminishes.

———————

Wakes were never just about the dead or the old gods. Dead is dead and a corpse has no shame, desire, fear or hope. Or manifests any form of belief in Hades, Valhalla, Heaven or Hell. You can't hurt its feelings. Nor cause it pain.

A corpse is indifferent to its nakedness, our anguish, and its fate, cremation in fire or rotting decay buried in earth. Or the joy or wreckage in the lives left behind.

We can blame the dead person for all sorts of things but their flaccid corpse no longer bears any earthly responsibility for the living. All his or her ages are gone, past tense, leaving behind just dry-ice-cold remains.

The biggest difference you notice for the first time in the company of the dead has nothing to do with whoever is in the coffin-shaped box. The real insight breaks out inside your head. Inside you.

Once you've got over the idea that you've not stumbled onto the set of a strange episode of some trick TV comedy series, and that there are no hidden cameras, it slowly begins to dawn that today's show is not even a show.

Or a unique occasion.

That the dead person is no one special. Not even a celebrity who has been on the TV so there is no excuse. Just another ordinary mortal. Like you. Nor is there a way to rewrite the script. Final. Forever.

There is a gentle, deflating but dawning realisation that you are now playing your own self in mortal reality where one by one all the characters die and the wider indifferent world goes on unchanged, unmoved, by this small drama of sequential extinction. And that one day the same small drama will happen to you too.

The Final thing can be hard to grasp at first because in the rest of life we go back on ourselves all the time. We pretend and lie countless times a day, often for good reasons.

'Your hair looks great; I don't think it even looks green at all.'

'This weekend? I'd love to but I've already got plans.'

'Absolutely, we'll do it.'

'I am just waiting on that other guy to come back to me.'

'It will be ready tomorrow.'

'No your arse does not look big.'

'I will always love you.'

We say cruel things and then apologise saying we never meant it and make up. We fail the test, resit, pass or fail again. Break something and buy a replacement. Promise to change and never do. Get a divorce then remarry.

Repair the roof after the storm. Damage something, or someone, and write out a cheque to make everything better. We strike a bargain, calculate the profit and the loss on the insurance claim and move on. We make up stories all the time about near misses, heroic deeds, inexplicable remissions and 'Hand of God' miracles that saved us while all around us the less worthy fell like mown grass.

We survive to live and lie another day. Sometimes most dangerously to ourselves.

But with the still cold dead lying in the box in front of you comes an alternative realisation – there is no reverse gear or miracle rescue from our mortality.

No amount of cardio pulmonary resuscitation, money, status, script rewrites, lies or belief will make this dead-person-thing sit up, cough and be alive again. Every word of their story is a past tense: what they did, where they lived, the right, the wrong, or how they got sick, who gave them what, the treatments they had and their final struggle, heroic or stoic.

Even the tragedy of a What-Never-Should-Have-Been, the fall on the stair step that was never seen, the bullet that never missed by those vital five millimetres, a childish accident in the paddling pool when the mother's back was turned for only so many few seconds, a teenage stabbing, a suicide attempt gone right, a misdiagnosis, the corona ventilator tube that was only blocked for a few minutes, cannot be undone by tears or love or anger.

All our stories end here and our true mortal powerlessness is inescapable.

Here now under the mortal sun, within grasp of your own warm flesh, is the objective defiance of every possibility-to-be. The very mirror of your own Death-to-Come.

And nothing on Earth will ever change that.

RULE FIVE: LEARNING HOW TO DIE IS THE SAME AS LEARNING HOW TO LIVE.

RULE FIVE

So what does that mean? Learning to die, learning to live?

Well the basic idea, once you've got over that first confrontation with a corpse, is just to start to learn to relax, lean into your mortality as they say, and get on with a few how-to-die courses. Which really are the same thing as how-to-live courses.

And recognise that dying is nothing special.

That does not mean you have to wear black, sleep in your coffin or visit graveyards every week. What it really means it that you start to learn to take the scariness out of death and don't feel so awkward around the dying or being mortal yourself given that you've no other options.

Remember **Rule Three** – how pretending to be immortal is a very bad idea?

But how can you do that? The death/life training bit? The not so scared bit?

Well you could begin with an Irish Wake.

When I was seven my mother took me to my first wake on the island for my first how-to-die lesson. The wake was in a small whitewashed cottage that was crammed with old ladies in black scarves and men wearing flat caps holding tobacco pipes and puffing away.

I was a grumpy child, bewildered by the strangeness of everything and the over-welcoming smiles of the adults around me. I slunk close behind my mother, holding her skirt, as she worked her way down the line of mourners in the small space surrounding the long box that was the coffin but which was too high for me to see into.

Ritually my mother shook the hands of what must have been the dead man's close family and repeated the same phrase: 'Sorry for your trouble.'

The Irish love children at funerals so even by my mother's side I was patted on the head, my cheeks squeezed and my looks complimented upon.

'A fine-looking *gasúr* [boy].'

I shrank away from these intruding strangers, even closer to my mother.

When we got to the head of the coffin, laid out on the kitchen table, my mother helped lift me up so I could peer over the side. I was too small to see by myself. Inside there was an old man with unnaturally yellow skin and sunken cheeks with dry barbed grey nostril hairs sticking out of his nose. He was lying on his back dressed in a brown suit and his yellow fingers, tobacco smoke stained, were clasped together and a set of grey rosary beads wrapped between them. I knew straight away that he was not alive. He was too still. I jerked away in revulsion back against my mother but she did not let me go.

On the other side of the coffin sitting down looking at us was a line of old ladies, eyes staring, smiling and grinning; it is a common Irish superstition that the prayers of a child, a sexual innocent, will rise quicker to Heaven for the benefit of the soul of the departed.

Whispering in my ear my mother said: 'Bless yourself and make a sign of the cross, Kevin, for the poor man's soul.' I made the Catholic sign of the cross, touching my forehead and chest and arms, muttering: 'In the name of the Father, and of the Son and of the Holy Ghost' to a chorus of silent grins from the old ladies watching.

Then my mother whispered again: 'Touch him, it will make you less afraid.'

So I reached into the coffin and ran the back of my hand against the dead man's cheek. I was shocked by the feel, cold, rubbery.

Seconds later, my mother let me drop back down on my feet and we moved along to join the seated ladies on the other side of the room and annoyingly chat away about lots of boring adult stuff. My death lesson was over.

In a few moments in the communal gathering of the Wake my mother had shown her son the very ordinariness of death. She was teaching me to embrace rather than fear the sight of the departed as death after all was nothing special. Within a few minutes another old lady brought over a plate and offered me a biscuit as a treat for being a good boy.

Nothing special? How much of a lesson was that?

Seeing a dead body as a seven-year-old was not the last of my death lessons but it was a start. Even as a child I was being shown a model of how to act at a wake, what to say and do, and most importantly how normal death was. I was being taught a little death-conquering.

Not everyone is going to get a chance to go to an island Irish wake but courses on learning how to conquer death are going on all around you in your town as well.

And as long as you are breathing you are qualified enough to start.

The best way to learn how-to-die properly is to get in on some live practice with the dying humans in your own neighbourhood. There are no better teachers.

Who else did you think could teach you? An academic? A priest? A counsellor?

All you need to do is pick up the phone or text and reach out. And then turn up.

Turn up? What does that mean?

No one can save the world but we can all in our personal lives use the small powers we do have to reach out to the dying, the bereaved, to break the Western denial of death.

So for instance when you hear that someone you know is sick or maybe dying why don't you just call them up and go visit?

Yes. Even if you don't know them that well. Or they have not sent you a formal invitation.

Is there anyone you know already, who you could visit?

Does the thought feel uncomfortable? Because it is just so awkward? Are you embarrassed about even the thought of making the call? What about texting? Would that make it easier? Or worse? Or are some things still too real to be shared across your iPhone screen?

But how can the thought of simply sending a text be more awkward than dying?

Why is the thought of just reaching out to the dying so problematic? So intrusive?

The reason for our squeamishness is the Western Death Machine. We have been subtly indoctrinated into believing that the minute the D-word is mentioned then the shutters have to come down, the curtains pulled across, and the dying isolated to their separate realm. We just know *somehow* the dying don't want us to intrude. We are certain of it.

Just as we know that the minute we hear about our own cancer diagnosis we will burn our address books, wipe our phones, and bar the front door because all we will really want to do is curl up in shame and die?

No we won't. It is not the shame of the dying but our fear of death that stops us reaching out, our denial. The dying generally really do want us there. As we would too.

We don't need to become another Mother Teresa picking out random dying strangers off the streets to integrate our life into their dying. But we could all start by rebooting our personal version of the Western Death Machine by going to visit that aged aunt who is in the old folks' home not so very far away.

Any loose mortal connection will do.

You could pop in on the old man down the corridor in your apartment block with the oxygen tubes in his nose. Ask if there is something you could do. Maybe help with the groceries?

Or go knock on the door of the mother of that girl you knew back home who killed herself, even though no one ever really knew why, who might just want a bit of company for an afternoon?

Or when you hear the news of a death, don't hesitate. Call your friends, your relatives, straight away, right at that moment wherever you are, to offer your condolences and let them ramble away on the phone as long as they want.

And then?

Go see them, maybe after that phone call, armed with a packet of biscuits and a couple of spare hours to listen and talk. What's the harm? What could possibly be more important in life than death? Your next business meeting? A Zoom call?

Yes but what would you talk about?

How about whatever the dying or bereaved person wants to talk about? That could be football, politics, the state of the world, the miracle cure they expect to receive at any moment, their ungrateful children, their bowels and bladder, their sex life, the laundry and the crosswords. Their loneliness. The exact words won't matter but the Being-There by you will.

Are you not convinced? Or do you feel those words of silent resistance inside your head? That little voice that says: 'I am just not going to do that.' Because you really are disgusted by the thought of being near the dying, bedpans, blood and death? The so-called indignity of it all.

Let's imagine it was the other way around and you were the one doing the dying.

Would you really rather be left alone to die all by yourself? The phone never ringing. Being shunned. Or being left to grieve alone because it was just too awkward to talk to you.

Or do you think you would be better off if there were people around? And someone came round to at least help out with the cooking?

If you do go visit the dying or the bereaved enough times, practice, practice, practice, you'll get over your own self-conscious awkwardness, your panic and fear, and start to relax.

You don't have to go out of your way but don't shun the opportunity to learn. There are a lot of jokes, great moments, in death and dying. And some great insights into the quiet courage, love and dignity of ordinary lives. Real people. And because there is nothing more real in life than death you will learn a lot.

Although it should come as no surprise, not everyone was born to be a star on daytime television. Or be hailed on the fleeting internet dial as a visionary, an entrepreneur, a CEO or a thought leader. A conversation starter. Or have a million-strong social media following.

Most of us, most often the best of us, will live out our lives in dedicated obscurity patiently turning up day after day at work and at home stopping the world falling apart bit by bit and not get much notice or reward for it. A nurse, a teacher, a delivery driver, a worker. Humble soldiers of everyday life with neither medals nor glory. The unheralded army of the Us.

The cult of celebrity we collectively worship consciously diminishes the value of those millions, of billions, of 'ordinary' lives.

Death teaches another story and in those final days it is possible to see clearly the strength and courageous tenacity, the flaws and failures, sometimes the sheer goodness, that has sustained an ordinary unrewarded soul in life.

On death's trail don't expect to meet too many saints. Or hear too many deathbed confessions. If you were a selfish bastard most of your life then chances are you'll be a selfish bastard in most of your dying too.

Being in pain, or being dosed up on opiates, can also get in the way of what you might be anticipating if you're expecting clear-sighted Stoic philosophical reflection on the meaning of life by the dying person.

Dying is also a self-centring act; the responsibilities of the living slip away from the dying person day by day as they medically negotiate their final days. Their horizon shrinks, a bed, a sitting room, and closes in around them. Their lives bleed out day by day. The dying sleep a lot.

Dying too is an exhausting process both for the soon-to-be-deceased and their carers. And this is where we can all prove ourselves useful, if only to relieve the immediate family or professional staff of their much greater burdens for a few hours.

You can run errands, pick up prescriptions, take the dog for a walk, make supper or clean the fridge. There will always be something that needs doing even if it's just watching TV together, sharing time, because this is what dying is really like, one small mundane act after another. Real life, messy, complicated, not the edited-down movie version.

Are you disappointed because it is not like in the films? With the doctors in scrubs and the CPR electrodes shouting, 'Clear!' The drama.

Don't worry. The realness of death will change your life in so many ways that no movie ever could. An experience you will carry with you until your own dying day long after all childish things, and last year's box set, are forgotten.

Because at last you will understand what it is to be truly human.

In the full Irish Wake tradition, no one dies alone; someone is always there to watch over them, a guardian of a kind, to be there at the moment of their death. That death vigil, exhausting as it is, is another act of grace and our first and last eternal wish. An act of love.

If to be born amidst a community who will love you is the first best hope of life then surely to die among those who love you still is the last best hope of life?

Would you not want that for yourself at least?

A loved ending rather than the coldness of a hired bed somewhere between the comings and goings of this night's shift rota on the fifth floor of the Memorial Something General Medical Ward?

Do you really want to die like former British prime minister Margaret Thatcher, once one of the most powerful people on the planet, who died alone among strangers as if forgotten, in a rented hotel room in the care of an agency nurse, almost as unloved as it is possible to be?

Or would you want someone you loved to be there for you watching over you at the end? A guardian to see you softly into death?

A proper death vigil is not something you can do alone, or even within the resources of a family, it takes time and energy and multiple bodies. Someone will have to be there, a watcher, even in the small hours of the night. The vigil needs the care and attention of the many not just the few.

Perhaps you could volunteer to take a watch just like one of our Neolithic ancestors did on the plain?

But what would you gain from such an act of witness?

Nothing and Everything.

Unless you are employed as a professional carer your wages will be non-existent, the hours antisocial, and the food poor to middling.

Why bother?

The Everything bit comes when you reach the end of that first existential lesson – so this is what it is like to be human. And die. The final act of an Other's life.

In the Western Death Machine we have come to see dying as an act of inconsequence. But real dying is important. Seeing the process, being there, will make the next time easier, more predictable, less fearful.

Experiencing other people's deaths is like an inoculation, a protective process, that helps you negotiate your way through life and your own future death.

A map for your own mortal road.

The ending of another's life cannot but provoke questions within your own.

Is this the way I want to live my life too? Is my life the one I wanted? This job, this house, this daily commute, this plan to do what? Is this what my life is all about? And how can I change it?

Is this the way I want to die?

Is all the noise, the passing daily news frenzy, the scandals, the stars, the scores, anything more than empty proceedings to beguile the time and fill vacant space before your own death?

They are important questions because death's proximity sharpens and focuses our own mortal possibility; we all only have one life and the choices we make will determine our purpose.

If you still feel uncomfortable about doing death close up then there is always the option of doing death at a little more distance. Maybe you could start checking out the local funeral notices to see how many recently dead people you know and get in the habit of going along: the wake if there is one, the funeral home, the church, the music, the service, the words said, or left unsaid, the grief and the tears. The family arguments. And the food and wine afterwards if you are invited.

You might feel like an imposter, a perfect stranger, but you do have a right to be there.

Remember the tolling bell of **Rule One?**

If the family did not want anyone to come to the funeral, why advertise the service? And by your presence you are showing respect for their dead relative, one of the Us.

Take up the invitation to go and, like the Irish, rate funerals as at least as important as wedding invitations on the social index.

Don't be afraid of being a voyeur; everyone is. You would not be human if you were not. Look and don't flinch away if you have come to discover death. Participate.

The worst funerals are no more than an empty ceremonial. The best are where the shields slip and you can see and feel a sorrow that pierces your heart and exposes a mortal wound.

Once on the island I was there in the funeral crowd in the church for a neighbour who had died of bowel cancer in her seventies. Her agonising death was long expected. 'A blessing', of a kind, as the islanders would say, that brought an end to her torment and muted the emotional temperature of her funeral.

Her long-anticipated demise before her death was an established fact, inevitable, and could not be regretted and her funeral Mass a further part of the set dry-eyed procedure. Except for when her nephew, a substitute son, who in the island tradition was one of her six pallbearers, began to weep uncontrollably, the tears running down his face without shame, as he carried her swaying coffin away from the altar and out of the church.

The rawness of the emotion, the pain of his loss and

love for her, rippled as a wave through the congregation in a gathering of tears, the biting of lips and a flood of feeling. In his reddened face, in the heaving sobs, her death was made real, the loss of her life reborn in sadness.

In the crowd we the watchers were cut to the quick, his grief igniting the memory of our own personal griefs for other deaths, in a collective sharing. A reminder of our common bond.

I am my Other sister's keeper.

Even in the midst of the coronavirus pandemic, when all social gatherings were banned and funerals curtailed to a few family members, villagers in rural Ireland quickly adopted a new way of showing their respect for the deceased by individually lining the funeral route, at a safe distance from each other, as the cortège passed through their town.

They denied the pandemic absolute dominion and conquered death again.

———

In Ireland getting a good turnout at your grandmother's funeral can be akin to winning big in the local amateur football league. The number of cars, the length of the tailback of the funeral cortège and the filling of the church with mourners are all seen as high scores and deemed endorsements of the social standing of the deceased, and their family, within the community. Of course, you can only win big if others fail and this Irish funeral rivalry provokes its own form of sardonic humour. Jokes are made about hardcore 'funeral hobbyists' whose entire hasty social life is planned around 'the deaths' schedule read out on local radio or pored over in the daily newspaper. And whose 'defensive wake-going' is seen as an insurance policy to ensure their own death nuptials will be well attended in turn.

Irish politicians too are often compelled by electoral necessity to attend the funerals of every dead constituent in order to retain the remaining votes of the deceased's relatives. Endorsed from the grave.

Even in death humans don't stop being self-interested. But the self-interestedness of the Irish around death is nothing like the dwindling cruelty of a Western Death Machine funeral where no more than two handfuls of aged mourners are ever likely to attend.

Of course, that is a generalisation and it is not always true. But it is also true you never need to count the cars and boast about the length of the cortège at most English and American funerals because in general hardly anyone ever goes to them. The dead are deemed valueless and so easily forgotten. And the grief of others a forbidden realm.

But why bother anyway? What have other people's deaths and funerals got to do with my life?

Turning death into a whisper would work if it made you immune from mortality but it doesn't.

Denial just robs you of an understanding, a familiarity with death, that makes life and mortality easier to navigate rather than finding yourself alone and terrified, plunging towards oblivion when death comes.

Learning how to die is the same as learning how to live because the two are indivisible.

RULE SIX: THE DEAD
ARE EVERYTHING AND
NOTHING LIKE US.

RULE SIX

A wake begins and ends in an existential confrontation between the living Us and a dead Us.

A body of a dead human laid out on a kitchen table, a sofa or in a lace-lined coffin in the front sitting room. Or a funeral home. A dead body you can reach out to and touch, hold their hand, ruffle their hair, even lips you can kiss.

If you have never seen or touched a human corpse and only watched the TV drama version, don't be surprised to discover that real dead people are nothing like actors pretending to be dead. But you might also be surprised how much you can learn about human existence, a complete degree in Death Studies, in just a few minutes of being in their company.

The real dead are everything and nothing like Us and the shock of that first encounter, in its sameness and differences, will be the most important lesson you ever learn in life.

Death is a mystery too. Relatives of the bereaved often struggle to articulate the utterness of difference between the living and the dead as if they can no longer reconcile the identity of the body they see before them with their memory of the living person.

People feel that the 'soul' of the person, the who they were, has disappeared. As if the great animating current of the deceased's personality has evaporated, leaving a vestige of their former being behind. The body is there but not the person.

This very difference between life and death is the basis of all religion, the hunger for eternal life, and has spawned innumerable priesthoods, temples, mosques, churches, empires, persecutions and religious conflicts. And millions of other deaths.

Deadness is important.

We scrabble around for the right words to explain what perceptually seems inexplicable but is just our own generational rediscovery of physical death. The shock is real. Tactile.

Every human you have ever touched before is a warm-blooded mammal. But the dead are so cold their flesh sears your lips.

When I first kissed my dead brother Bernard in his coffin the fridge-like chill of his forehead made me instinctively question if my brother had been replaced by a perfectly carved block of stone. This marble-cold facsimile, down to the individual freckles on his face, could never have been human so therefore could never have been my brother. Except it was him.

'How could you do that?'

'Kiss him?'

'Never mind touch him.'

'Agh, I never want to see that.'

'I want to remember my mother as she really was.'

'I'd get nightmares for the rest of my life.'

'What about catching something?'

Disgust. It is one of our primordial protective responses to rotten meat, contagion, faeces, other people's bodily fluids, vomit and dead things.

'That's disgusting, blah, blah.'

The word slips so easily off the tongue. But disgust is a cultural creation too. We are disgusted all the time at those we regard as sexual deviants, the unwashed poor, kids with snot on their faces, or those of a contrary political persuasion even as our definition of deviancy changes like the tide.

Somewhere in the last two generations we've attached disgust to all dead humans too. We've invented a biological myth that the second someone stops breathing permanently they become a rancid decomposing mass of pathogens, Ebola, corona or something like it, which will kill you just by being in the same room.

A myth first invented by American undertakers keen to sell clients their 'hygienic' US$1,000 corpse-embalming package, which replaces your blood with a toxic mix of formaldehyde, dye and other embalming fluids.

The coronavirus pandemic has only exacerbated this fear even when the cause of death, like cancer, is clearly not a contagion.

Conveniently too, but profoundly, we've lost all sense of control of our right to the possession of the dead body of our loved one, believing that all sorts of laws and regulations now exist on health and safety grounds, even when they don't, to prevent the imminent outbreak of bubonic plague or anything like an Irish Wake at home.

A falsity that we have now readily taken up to justify our further total avoidance of the sight of the dead in the Western Death Machine. Fear.

Fear? Well how many dead bodies have you seen?

Touched?

Or kissed?

One? Two? Three? Your grandmother? Aged parent?

Can you even count the dead you've seen on the fingers of more than one hand?

Is that not strange the number is so few given that the overall mortality rate for humans is a hundred percent? Why has the sight of the dead become so rare, so privileged, so intimate and so taboo?

In Ireland, the sight and touch of the dead would be, because it is, an every-other-day occurrence. From their childhood onward an ordinary person, wake after wake, would have seen dozens, maybe hundreds of bodies by the time they reach middle age. And if the Irish see and touch dead bodies all the time and don't drop dead *en masse* then the problem is not the corpse but our Western death denial. The Machine.

A wake in Ireland usually begins at the moment of death and most people are buried within three days, so even in summer there is no real need to embalm a body. Nor will a body decay in such a short time frame.

There is nothing but our own will, or ignorance, that prevents us seeing the bodies of those we love. And if you can't bury someone in that time frame there is always the option of the undertaker's mortuary fridge as you wait for the mourners to gather.

You might be asking yourself why you should be with the dead.

I'm not Irish. I don't want to see any dead bodies. Why should I?

But why should you not? What part of you is not part of the Mortal Us?

And there is so much to learn.

Do you remember that game you played as a child pretending to be dead? Holding your breath, trying not to fidget? Or if you were doing the watching, waiting for that tiny intake of breath or a little flicker of the closed eyes that gave the game away?

Now pretending to be dead is a game the deceased are truly hopeless at. They are great at being dead but hopeless at the 'pretending to be something else' bit. And that everything and nothing difference is important.

The dead exist in another state of Being, Deadness. But it is a state of Being, another form of humanness, that we cannot, however hard we try, conjure away into nothingness.

When you look at them – the dead – in their coffin they have an eerie immobility. Not a flicker. No 'real' person could ever pretend to be so still.

The dead too are stubbornly indifferent. You can howl in rage, weep buckets of tears, hold them in your hands and whisper in their ears how much you love or hate them and they don't react. Ever.

It is confusing, like you are talking to a human-shaped stone. Or a dead person.

Dead human flesh too has a strange unhuman flaccidity. An ice-cube-in-a-rubber-glove feeling when you press on their cheeks and meet a numb fathomless lack of resistance or response. Poking the dead is like prodding the flesh of a whole uncooked chicken in the fridge.

And here is another existential epiphany – the dead don't look well.

Live humans are meaty inflated balloons of blood, bone, muscle and skin. Even as you are reading this book your heart is pumping blood round your arteries at just under three pounds per square inch of pressure. The pressurised blood fluffs up your face, makes your cheeks rosy and fills the veins in your hands.

But when the pump stops the pressure stops too and gravity takes over. All the blood drains away from the face and head and pools in the lower back or limbs. Cheeks sag hollow and your face looks thinner. The fingers of the dead turn a bloodless yellow-ivory colour. If you are black- or brown-skinned you lose colour too and look greyer, paler.

In fact you look dead.

Hypocrisy and lying often get a bad press but they can be very useful tools, small kindnesses, in the company of the deceased. To fill these voids of deadness the Irish have invented a fairly specialised vocabulary as they slip past the open coffin reassuring relatives of the deceased that their loved ones are still high up there in the corpse beauty league.

'I'd say she's looking grand.'

'God your mother always had lovely hair.'

'You wouldn't think he is a day over fifty.'

'Sure all the pain of the cancer has gone from his face.'

'He's looking like himself again.'

Small lies, harmless compassions, in the openness of the wider truth of death's encounter.

***

Cold. Still. Indifferent. Flaccid. Bloodless. The dead.

The everything and nothing like Us yet who still remain, because they are, a perfect record of those we have loved.

The indivisible 'was' and 'is' of Them. Separate from us by a thousand incongruities and the absoluteness of this mortal division. A wonder and a puzzlement here in the flesh. Now truly our Other.

Those remains, the bodies of the dead, matter still for the sight and knowing of all that was lost.

When you love someone in life, a son, a wife, you don't stop loving them and their body just because they died. The memory of the dead lingers on inside us long after they have gone. Even decades later it is common to 'talk' to the dead inside your mind and act out their perceived wishes. Grief.

If you are ever there in the room with someone you love who happens to be dead and some fool says something about their dead body 'just being a shell', feel free to softly slap that living idiot somewhere just so they remember never to say the same hurtful crass death-denying lie again.

Or if you are not an angry person you could offer to be ready to throw their dead body in the garbage truck within minutes of their death because after all they will 'just be a shell' then too.

We need the bodies of the dead as a focus for our grief and love and to see and know the transition from the living 'who' to the dead 'was'. To see and experience their other state of Deadness, if only to convince ourselves of that fact.

Why do you think our foremothers, in the keens of grieving, invested so much energy in these stages of leaving if not to teach and heal?

———

In our new Western death tradition of denial, the sick and dying never really die, they disappear. One day they are walking the Earth, or sick in bed, and then something happens and you never see them again, ever.

The following-on dislocated ceremonials, the closed wooden box, a grave, a crematorium, weeks after they have disappeared, are just outward symbols, tokens of hollow passage for the common dead.

Can you ever be certain the being you loved is in the box?

This shielding away from death begins long before the last breath in the way we remove the dying from our sight, usually into our local hospital where they are swiftly swallowed inside the Western Death Machine. Before their body cools they disappear inside closed trolleys to discreetly located mortuaries and windowless black undertaker vans.

Their death is defined by their absence rather than their dead presence.

The saddest funeral I ever attended was an old university friend who had hidden his terminal illness from everyone except his strange narcissistic wife. We had been close in our thirties and I had enjoyed his wry cynical view of life and his take on the pomposities of office and ambition.

Andrew was a man who had nursed his mother in her dying day and so he was hard to fool about the inflated glories of the so-called great and powerful.

As is common, through no one's real fault, we had drifted apart in middle life, different pathways, children, family, but I remembered him very fondly. So it was a jolting surprise to receive an email invitation to Andrew's funeral.

The next time I met Andrew he was in a squarish small box, 50 centimetres by 60 centimetres, in the grounds of a freezing cold modern concrete tomb of a church in February in Scotland and being held up in the arms of the female vicar as if she was holding a cigar box and potentially offering them to members of the congregation.

Except of course it wasn't Andrew, just his ashes; his body had been cremated long before this peculiar funereal rite. His literal diminishment felt grotesque. His wife, his sole seeming confidante, seemed obliviously happy at being the centre of attention and the recipient of repeated condolences. It was she who had trawled every old address book to gather in her dead husband's oldest friends for this peculiar parting.

For an hour we gathered in a constructed ceremonial of remembrance holding small candles in the gloom, whose wax dripped on fingers and pews before expiring.

I was not alone in being gripped by an uncertainty as to the 'who' we were remembering. Andrew's illness, a withering but swift cancer, had been a secret kept from family, colleagues at the accountancy firm, everyone, as if his dying was an act of shame.

Speaker after stunned speaker from his family, his work, at the altar mouthed the same visceral shock at being here in this simultaneous moment of suffering the pain of his loss and enacting his solitary burial.

Underpinning the altar homilies was the same unspoken thought and unrequited anger – did Andrew believe no one loved him?

We are all free to choose how to live and how to die; denying you are going to die is a common coping mechanism and a common lie. Andrew was free to manage his own death, and who he told about his illness, in whatever way he chose, as we all are. What he couldn't do was entirely divorce himself from the tolling bell of the universal Us or the aftermath in his going.

Some of his old friends had travelled halfway across Europe to be at his funeral, yet we all felt as we had been invited to a lavish party where the mysterious host never appears and the guests are left wondering what is going on.

Why have a funeral at all if you had freely sought your own oblivion unburdened by the potential concern of others?

Unvoiced was both our collective regret and our anger at what felt like deceit by either his wife or Andrew and the wife together. Why did Andrew not get back in touch?

Was our old friend the same man as the man who had denied us all our friendship or any insight or care, or possibility, of being part of his dying days? Why did he not reach out to say goodbye?

But Andrew was dead and there was no one to ask for the answer. I left the church chilled in the sadness of the loss and the irresolution.

I keep the card of his memorial service pinned on a noticeboard at home but every time I see Andrew's picture with his sad resigned smile – seemingly knowing he was dying – I wonder did I ever know this stranger?

I wonder too about the last months of his life. How lonely they must have been holding the secret of his coming death from everyone around him.

Why?

In denying his coming death in shame Andrew denied us too, turning his back on family and friends, all of whom had at different times shared his life journey. He denied the Us. The finality, the cruelty, of his decision cannot be reversed.

Nor is he alone. Such death shame is increasingly common. For a myriad of different often difficult, sometimes unfathomable, reasons many individuals in the Western Death Machine feel unable to say out loud that they have a terminal illness; that they are dying.

Sometimes people say they do so because want to 'protect' their children. Or they don't want colleagues to know – as if mortality was some kind of shameful sexual infection. A weakness that will be exploited by others?

Or that their Stage 4 cancer diagnosis is some form of hush-hush negotiation whose very existence must be shielded so as to prevent its actualisation. Or that dying is their own private business and they don't want other people knowing their secrets.

But lying about your coming death is not a means of protecting anyone, particularly a child, from harm. Or yourself.

Death will overtake the denial and become a truth.

Abstracting death from 'normal life' is like abstracting the concept of gravity from the surface of the Earth. It is impossible.

All the lies, elisions, contradictions, just add an additional burden in those final days and on the bereaved when you finally stop breathing and your deadness is non-negotiable.

What great secret are you withholding in the first place? Your special place among the mortal Everyone?

We are all stronger, less fearful, when we can stand looking up at the oncoming on the far horizon together rather than treading along alone in fear, looking down, just waiting for the ground beneath our feet to swallow us up.

Such death shame would be anathema to our ancestors who recognised death as an inevitability and saw the rite of burial as a set of obligations between the living and the dead.

How can I expect my people to care enough to bury me if I don't care enough about my dying to tell them in the first instance? If those mortal Others have no claim upon me?

Whose responsibility is death? It may seem strange but if you don't teach your children how to die then who do you expect will teach them?

The last thing my father Sonny taught me and the rest of his children on the island when he was terminally ill with pancreatic cancer was one of life's oldest lessons: how to die.

It was his last parental lesson, which he did humbly with great grace and an unwavering courage. He accepted his death because he had no other choice.

In an Irish Wake that death responsibility becomes a communal rite and an unspoken social obligation. We gather together to bury an individual but also to gather in a younger generation to teach and educate them about our collective mortality one small death step at a time.

We share our deaths for a wider purpose because the *we* of the community is always greater, more enduring, than any one individual. We follow on from those who have died before stretching back past the gates of Troy and beyond.

My death, like my life, is just part of a wider story, not the ending but the going on. What after all could be more human?

The Western Death Machine, seeing death only as an individual trauma, no longer recognises these social obligations. We are erasing death's ceremonial presence in our lives, as if like death, itself, such rituals have no substance or meaning.

Direct cremations, where the body of the dead is shipped without ceremony direct from the hospital to the nearest crematorium and returned as a Fed-Ex package of ashes, are on the rise.

So too is the no-funeral funeral where a line of death notice text, 'At Mr X's request there was no funeral,' in a local paper is substituted for a public ceremony.

The bells of common humanity are silenced.

No wonder we have found ourselves in trouble with grief.

A bodiless death, the elision of an end ritual, is like digging a black hole in the universe that is harder to fill because in the shock of bereavement we are never really sure where the body of our loved one went.

Or what happened. How the world has altered forever.

In shunning the physicality of the dead we deny ourselves one of the most important therapeutic powers of the Wake. In life we touch each other all the time, mothers and sons, children, parents, lovers, handshakes with newfound strangers, and the guiding arms of passers-by.

In our Western denial we never even begin to complete what our ancestors saw as their overwhelming obligation: the close possession of the body of their beloved dead until it was safely laid in earth or cremated, the laying to rest. The rite of burial.

We have swapped such tactile guardianship for industrial dispossession. Every night of the life before the body of your loved one, their being, slept in a bed at home or in hospital.

In death that same body is instantly reassigned as nothing more than a carcass to be stored somewhere unknown awaiting disposal whenever the bureaucrats at the local crematorium can schedule a slot for burning.

Where do the bodies of our dead go in between?

Such is the overwhelming power of the Western Death Machine that this abnegation of the bodies of the dead, the dislocation between the dying and the burial of the who you loved, is never challenged but acquiesced to as if it was inevitable.

Why? Whose dead body is this? Whose grief?

Is it any wonder our unburied dead come back to us in our dreams? Sometimes our nightmares.

So why do we deny ourselves the knowledge, and tender comfort, of seeing the beauty of what is gone? The comfort of a dead mother, son, daughter in your arms? Your father, mother, lover, child, never existed without this body. The same body now laid out in a coffin or on a bier whose flesh can be touched, held and wept over as the focus of your love. Or your anger. Here in transit on this way station of final days.

———

I kissed my dead brother because I loved him still even in the agony of that moment of loss.

How could I deny either myself or him?

Our dead truly are the Everything and Nothing like Us. Why then in fear do we deny ourselves the right to say goodbye?

RULE SEVEN: THE PLEASURE OF THE SORROW OF TEARS.

RULE SEVEN

Intrinsic to the Wake, hidden within its surface rituals, is a whole host of what we would now term therapeutic practices for healing the living. The Trojans, the Egyptians, the Greeks, the Jews, the Aztecs, the Irish all hired professional keeners, female mourners, to howl, wail and lament over the body of the deceased and provoke an emotional catharsis among family members. An outpouring of grief.

Professional keeners for hire are still a part of funerals in Africa, India and Asia even today. In Ghana you can hire a whole squad of mourners and choose from a menu of options with the deluxe keening version, 'crying, insulting other mourners for their lack of emotion, rolling on the ground and threatening to jump into the grave' costing around US$100.

Our ancestors saw no shame in such public sorrow. The Wake is a stage where grief is licensed and applauded both for men and women. The higher the status of the dead the greater the lamentation, paid or unpaid, to signify the value of the loss to the family and the community. These keeners, 'minstrels of the dirge', enable the other mourners to channel their grief.

In *The Iliad* Achilleus, maddened by grief for the loss of his lover Patrokolos, encourages his soldiers, the Myrmidons, to scream and lament around Patrokolos' body, driving their chariots round and round until 'the sands and the men's armour are wet with tears'. Achilleus, the greatest ancient Greek hero, urges his war-loving companions on until 'we have had the fill of our pleasure in the sorrow of tears.'

Achilleus, like a grief counsellor, was seeking to evoke an emotional catharsis in his soldiers.

Strikingly, Achilleus' keening, his tears, are never portrayed by Homer as a sign of weakness or frail femininity but the actions of a feared warrior.

There is no shame in grief before the gates of Troy.

In contrast, we are disturbed by the power of such unshielded emotion. 'Don't cry,' so to speak.

We shy away from such directed emotional outbursts fearing that in the crying out, in the giving in to grief and wailing out, the chaos of death will overwhelm us. That we will be driven mad by a few howls and tears and never regain control of our minds. That in 'breaking down', a woman or a man weeping openly at a funeral, we will be overcome, conquered, by death. And that for our sanity and social propriety we must always internalise our emotions.

But why not cry, why not howl, and tear your hair, beat your breast and lament the loss of love and share in a collective outpouring of sorrow? If not now within sight of your dead then when? Why not scream out our sorrow?

What are we afraid of?

At my father's wake on the island, his sisters, daughters and female relatives gathered around his coffin as the principal mourners to call out over his corpse. Their tears, and keens, were infectious. The cry of one woman induced a cry in another. If another close relative arrived there would be a further burst of weeping and a flood of tears.

Over time, and continued repetition, the emotional intensity waned, drained out, as we had our fill of weeping. The public ceremonial quickened and intensified the grieving ritual.

The purging of emotion was also a collective act, a bonding together. Far from losing their minds the unity of the keening chorus bound the wounds of the bereaved up inside their community.

Is it not blindingly obvious, and more psychologically healing, that it is safer to cry together than cry alone? Each woman's individual pain and loss was demonstrably felt by others, a psychic unity, that hardened too into an irrevocable acceptance of my father's deadness.

I wept too.

The elision of 'wanting to remember them as they really were', the denial of the sight of the dead, has a price.

Where our ancestors vented, we suppress, internalising grief that corrosively leaches out in silence. The bereaved live inside themselves spectators at their own funereal feast, an alienation that carries its own psychological toll.

A common grief reaction is to believe, somehow, that the dead will return once everything settles down after the blur and business of their funeral.

An unconscious expectation of a magical reappearance that dogs the griever and manifests itself in untouched bedroom shrines, wardrobes filled with now never-to-be-worn clothes and a refusal to move house lest the returning dead become lost and bewildered at finding strangers in the old family home.

The mourner is left marooned in their grief unable to fully relinquish their dead, to cleave themselves away from what was and build a changed self. They walk through life buried in the invisible shroud of the deceased, every encounter filtered, even poisoned, by what is not.

A wake, or some such ritual, in its vehement spectacle of the deadness of the deceased makes such a subconscious haunting more difficult to conjure. The public passages of a wake, the body, the vigil, the communal gathering, are physically imprinted memories that are not so easily magically erased from the mind of the bereaved.

In Ireland, each mourner at the funeral too is under a social imperative to shake the hands of the bereaved and offer their personal condolences. 'Sorry for your trouble', 'Sorry for your trouble', repeated and repeated.

So many people shake the hands of the bereaved that your hands begin to hurt and Irish undertakers advise their clients to take their wedding and other rings off to prevent bruising.

The phrase itself is delivered at the same moment as the hand of the mourner is gripping the hand of the bereaved. In the undertow each mourner, like a muscle memory, is reinforcing the same existential message: 'They are dead, they are dead, they are dead, they are dead, and they are not coming back.'

In contrast to our Western silencing of death, the Irish are under a social obligation to publicly acknowledge the loss of the deceased to the bereaved the first time they meet after the death.

For months after the burial the same muscular reinforcement of deadness is repeated in public, in the office, in the street or in any chance encounter in the supermarket or bar.

'Sorry for your trouble' is the favoured phrase but the words are tokens of a further persistent public confirmation of the reality of the bereavement and the legitimacy of grief.

Unconsciously, the wake, the noise and the rituals, forces all of its participants forward into an acceptance of an irrevocable change of state. The dead are never coming back. But nor are they to be forgotten.

Our ancestors dealt with their grief by giving licence to its raw public exposure both at the wake and also in further rituals of remembrance months and years afterwards.

Shrines to the ancestors, weekly visits to the grave, prayers and offerings at their tombs, Salat-al-Janazah, Dia De Los Muertos, Cemetery Sundays, where family graves are annually cleaned before a special ceremony of remembrance is said, are all instances of a whole catalogue of rituals for the dead that exist in all of the world's religions as a formal means of signifying loss and the validity of the public expression of grief.

But who visits the dead now? Do we even know where our great-grandparents lie buried?

We no longer bury our dead. In Europe and North America over seventy percent of the dead are now burned not buried, cremated. A shortage of graves, cost, convenience and adapting custom and practice have all shifted the very physicality of the existence of the dead. We diminish death further.

In our modern ritual of cremation, and mandated cremulation – the grinding into dust of any bones not consumed in the furnace – we have both physically and psychologically disembodied the dead and substituted instead a homeless bag of ashes. There is nowhere to go for a rite of remembrance. A paid-for little brass plaque on the crematorium wall, among the hundreds, is not a tomb of anyone.

Like us the ancient Romans burned their dead but also entombed the cremated remains. The dead still had a physical place in the world set beyond the boundaries of the city. A dwelling point that could be visited. Without a grave, or a locus, it is easy to see why our dead are both nowhere and everywhere, erupting unbidden from that graveyard of lost souls we are now forced to carry within us.

Why are we surprised that we are so troubled by modern grief when we have abandoned every device our ancestors used to release, control and contain the most powerful emotions we will ever feel?

––––––––

For the mourner, the wake and the funeral too can and should be a mortal renewal of the pleasures of sorrow, and the joy of being alive.

It is okay to be sad about someone else's death and self-ishly glad you are still alive, like Achilleus' soldiers and their tears for Patrokolos.

That your closeness to another's death is a renewal because you have survived to die another day.

You shouldn't feel guilty.

I went to a funeral of a male friend in London who died young, in his early fifties. Bowel cancer. It was sad. His daughter, in her early twenties, who he was close to, was losing her dad and all the support he could have given her in the life to come.

The Never-Nevers.

Never to walk her down the aisle on the day of her marriage. Never to see his grandchildren. Now she was an only child alone in the world. An orphan.

Stephen had had the usual ups and downs. He was estranged from his first wife – who had left him even when their daughter was young – but had a new partner. So for the partner too there was the loss of all those What-Could-Have-Beens.

Stephen had been sick for three years but he didn't want anyone outside his immediate family involved in his dying. He fended off offers of help. Sometimes that is the way it goes. Unlike Andrew, Stephen did tell everyone he was dying.

Stephen had worked in lots of different jobs, editing, magazines, running a bar, and always been a great raconteur. A good man to share stories with and he seemed to know lots of people across a whole raft of interests. The crematorium was packed, two hundred or more.

In the ending of his days Stephen had become a bit of a Buddhist so there was lots of Eastern music and prayers to Gaia, the Earth goddess, at the ceremony and he had a closed wicker coffin.

Stephen's daughter gave a speech and a lot of people cried. And then a few of his friends also spoke. One of them broke down and cried at the microphone. It was okay to be upset, emotional, teary.

And then afterwards we all went to a local pub on the River Thames and drank cold white wine and ate canapés and people told stories about Stephen and laughed.

The sun was so strong that a few people got sunburned just from sitting around in the pub garden as the afternoon rolled along and the drink got drunk.

It was the height of summer so even after I left around eight and got home the air was still balmy, the clouds in the sky reflecting back the evening light like a mirror.

I was with someone I loved so we opened another bottle of cold wine and sat in a small back London garden in the dying light swinging on an old tatty hammock. At our feet was a cast-off child's paddling pool filled with cold water.

The summer heatwave had killed off the grass and the garden wasn't in great shape, a patchy beaten brown plot of nothing. And my life wasn't in great shape either; a lot of things I had wanted to happen that year hadn't and money was tight. I was feeling I was failing in middle age.

But there was a delicious contrast in the coldness of the paddling water on my foot and the sultry air with the sounds of the city, honks of traffic and the evening calls of children from the street and the rustle of leaves, as the light faded into darkness and the sun fled west.

I was alive and Stephen wasn't and I was glad I was here to savour this moment.

Part of me was sad about Stephen, full of regret, but another part of me was selfishly happy that I had survived to lie in this hammock and let the memories of this day – the day we burned Stephen – wash right through me: the incense, the speeches, the tears and the jumble of conversations.

Stephen's funeral, the closeness of my contact with his death, the grief of this irrevocable day, was a jolt, an inoculation of mortality against life's self-centred deceits.

My own petty failures were just that – petty. It was okay just to be alive.

How many others, throughout the long road of human history, had shared the same thoughts of middle-aged disquiet and worried over money? The schemes of things that had or had not come to pass? Keeping score on a self-indulgent perceived index of human happiness?

I was no one special, just lucky to be still here breathing.

Death teaches that what we see as success or failure in life are often arbitrary tokens of worth. Stripped of our illusions, most of us turn out to have the same sorts of desires, talents, needs, wants as most other human beings. We have successes, failures, happy or unhappy marriages, make mistakes and sometimes recover, are kind and cruel, brave and fearful.

Our lives are hedged in uncertainty, doubt, sometimes pain, deficits that we hide away from the rest of the world because we feel ashamed or think that others will see us as weak. Or we want to believe in our own dream.

Sometimes for good reasons, and sometimes for bad ones, we lie and most often present a version of ourselves to others that will we believe influence them in our favour. Make them envy us. Happy families. Blessed lives. Honesty will never be a virtue of Facebook.

We want to live in the gaze of others as greater, more loved, or more powerful, than we are. It is a desire as old as the first kings of Babylon who built palaces to their own glory and demanded that their subjects approach on their knees. For the multitude to look up not down at us even if the score is measured in nothing more than click likes and digital followers.

Death is our ultimate leveller. We are all corpses in the grave, stripped of any further worries about Twitter followers or our Facebook status. Or responsibilities.

Every Could-Have-Been has solidified into a Never-Was. Purported success, purported failure, whatever the measure of life, has come and gone; the dead are beyond our reach.

But we are also free to judge and recognise that the ordinary dead in their myriad fallibilities and strengths are no different from ourselves. Just human, all too human, like us.

Imperfect. Bound not by the make-believe and pretences of our projected self but by the compromises, irresolutions and definitions of time and place of our real lives.

Accepting yourself as yourself for yourself is death's most important lesson in life.

———

In the 1933 black-and-white talking movie *Queen Christina*, the Swedish actress Greta Garbo plays a thwarted cross-dressing seventeenth-century Swedish monarch who relinquishes her throne after a torrid affair with the Spanish ambassador Don Antonio, played by John Gilbert, a one-time star of the silent screen, who is now virtually forgotten.

Queen Christina is Hollywood made-up history but there is a powerful scene of memory where Garbo goes around the country inn bedroom, where the lovers first discover each other, touching every object. Don Antonio

asks what she is doing and she confesses that she is memo-
rising the room. 'In the future, in my memory, I shall live
a great deal in this room.'

Already her character, the queen, knows this love is
doomed even as it begins. Snowbound by a storm, and
fooled by her mannish disguise, her new lover Don
Antonio is unaware that the woman he has just slept with
is the unobtainable Swedish queen, and the zenith of their
love has already passed.

Later on his character will be killed in a pointless love
duel. Happiness will never come.

The movie, with its dreamy close-ups of the 28-year-
old Garbo's face, is a Hollywood classic, one of Garbo's
greatest roles, and was both a critical and commercial
success. The official MGM trailer for the film heralded
Garbo's return to the screen as – 'The Talk of the World'.
Garbo herself was paid US$300,000, a small fortune in
1933, to star in the film and was later nominated three
times for an Oscar as Best Actress.

On screen in the make-believe country inn, Gilbert
and Garbo still shine with a luminescent glory, forever
young, as two innocent snowbound lovers oblivious to
the coming tragedy that will engulf both their characters.
All we see is the moment. The aftermath is all to come.

We are often dazzled too by the seeming certainty of
the success of others like Garbo and Gilbert on the screen
of life before us. The seeming stars of today, or those we

envy, who seem to have all the glory, attention, the love and prizes we long for.

Will we ever have, like them, the life we wanted? Dreamed of? Or will we be denied it and fail? Will we even get to 'live' at all?

We are gnawed at by our own death anxiety. What is going to happen to me?

In *Queen Christina* not all the doom was screenbound. In real life Gilbert's film career was on the wane. Garbo and Gilbert had been lovers and he was given the part only on her insistence. His personal life was a mess; he flitted through four hasty marriages, a considerable fortune and drank himself to death in 1938 aged forty-one.

In the same year Garbo's own career crashed as she became 'box office poison.' She made her last film in 1941 and lived most of the rest of her life as a melancholic recluse, dying in 1990.

Happiness never came in real life either for the doomed queen and her lover.

When we look at the lives of others, and ourselves, it is hard to judge from wherever we stand if we will be happier or sadder or less or more fulfilled. We have no real knowledge of the future tears and fears of our own selves, or the endings of others, never mind old movie stars.

Or the moment of your death.

But that is okay. For if I were dead like Stephen would any of my own self-perceived failures, my mortal anxieties, matter at all? Or yours?

How great would it be to have been the real-life John Gilbert, despite the glamour of his Don Antonio character on screen? The glory, the adulation, the money, he burned through?

Does it sound harsh when I say I was glad to be alive in Stephen's death?

Or is it just a recognition of what we all feel but can't say because we are afraid to be so human?

In the dead, in the physical ending of them and their dreams, it is easier to forgive ourselves too for our own mortal limitations. To gain a true measure of what it is to be truly human.

In that tatty hammock, in the falling light of a London evening, I was embedded in the pleasure of sorrow, the heightened remembrance of the thrill and fragility of life.

It is one of the most important lessons the dead teach us.

Don't forget to forgive yourself in the pleasures of sorrow, the fatal joy of being alive, because one day for sure you won't be.

RULE EIGHT: TAKE
THE WEIGHT.

RULE EIGHT

On the mountain Slievemore on the island where the villagers bury their dead, the last act of obligation between the living and the dead comes in the final moments of burial. Professional pallbearers are unknown on the island and the coffin is always carried on the shoulders of the dead person's household: sons, nephews, sometimes neighbours.

Being carried to the grave by your sons is an old tribal Irish wish. A vivid proof that you were fertile, had issue, and are still revered enough in death to be borne aloft by your own kin, as your ancestors were to the same burial ground. That the circle of your life was fulfilled and you did not die alone, cast out.

The mountain is steep and the bulky weight of the coffin treacherous but this carrying 200 metres on the shoulders of six men, collarbone bruised, is regarded as an honour, an act of communal brotherhood. Even if there is a short-age of sons, there is never a shortage of volunteers.

Once they reach the open grave the coffin is placed over the hole but rests on three thick wooden stays. Underneath the coffin stretch three ropes and each pall-bearer, three on each side of the grave, then takes up the ropes in their hands and awaits the final command.

The digging of the grave too is another act of honour and is carried out for no payment by a volunteer band of village men led by the chief gravedigger, who oversees these burial rites. As the last prayers are said for the soul of the deceased the chief gravedigger calls out to the pall-bearers: 'Take the weight.'

Each man will then strain on their ropes and lift the coffin inches up and off the wooden stays – which are then pulled away by other gravediggers. For a few moments the full weight of the coffin and the dead body within sways in mid-air above the open grave held aloft only by the ropes wound round the pallbearers' now straining hands.

And then slowly, ever so slowly, each of the six men will let the rope slip inch by inch in unison through their hands, keeping the coffin level, lowering the full weight down and down to the bottom of the grave. It can be an ordeal, keeping time, the rope burning its way down through your fingers, marking flesh. Once the coffin rests on the floor of the grave the ropes are pulled free.

Before the eyes of the gathered mourners, the grave will be filled in by those gravediggers and, if the family so wishes, by the pallbearers too.

The sound of the earth hitting the coffin, the clash of the metal edge of the shovel blade digging into the earth, the clatter of tools shaping and levelling the mound of the grave is itself another haunting ritual.

So this is how another life, our life, ends in eternity and burial done.

In rain, in sunshine or storm, the same rite has been enacted on this windswept mountain for thousands of years as each generation returns to mark the same passage out of one of their own.

A stone forest of ageing bleaching gravestones, those Neolithic tombs, all mark out those who have gone before but also affirm the transcendence of the living community: he dies, she dies, but we, the living Us, never dies.

The past lives on in us, in the gathered, far more than we realise, like a familiar mooring in life's storm.

We need such familiar pathways and rituals to shape the stories of life's purpose and remind ourselves we are not alone, nor the first or the last to have endured. The union of the six pallbearers in the lowering of the coffin into the grave while keeping the coffin level is a perfect example of the communal endeavour that underpins the entire rite of the Wake. Each participant relies on the other to play their part, none can undertake the task alone. But in collectively taking the weight they all lessen the individual burden.

It takes a village to bury a woman or a man. And raise a child.

'Taking the weight' in the Irish Wake is not just something that happens only at the grave.

Those rafts of obligations begin long before the dying. Villagers, neighbours, family go out of their way to visit the sick and dying to say goodbye. There is none of the death shunning of the Western Death Machine. The islanders embrace the sick openly acknowledging that death is close and now is the time to say goodbye.

When else could they say goodbye?

Because the social space around death in Ireland is louder, like the daily roll call of the dead read out on the local radio, the private space around dying is wider too. It is easier to talk about death.

Many of these death calls to a dying neighbour are, on the surface, no more than social visits, the asking after your health, which allows the dying the freedom to either openly acknowledge their coming death or if they so wish maintain some form of personal death denial.

In their final days far-flung relatives of the soon-to-be deceased are called to return home to gather at the death-bed. Close neighbours join in the death vigil taking turns in the night to watch over the dying person even if they are in a coma. No one is allowed to die alone among strangers.

Traditionally after death the body is washed by local women, *Bean Cabhrach*, the old-fashioned layer-outer who in the past also doubled as a midwife.

Sometimes the family wash the body themselves; my sister under instruction from my aunt, a *Bean Cabhrach* herself, washed my father's body, closing the mouth by wrapping a bandage round the head and placing heavy coins on the eyelids to ensure they were shut.

As with so many other rituals of the Wake, the knowledge of caring for the dead is passed down from generation to generation by practice not a textbook.

Undertakers too have a role in the Wake. Who else will sell you a coffin or rent you a hearse in rural Ireland? But the role of an Irish undertaker is very different from the encompassing grip of an English or American undertaker where through the hospital, the mortuary, the long delay between death and burial, a professional layer of bureaucrats retain possession of the body and therefore dictate the death process. He who controls the body controls death.

Without a body there can be no wake, no open encounter between the generations of the living and their future mortality, no learning, no vigil and no transcendence of death. A true Wake begins at death with the corpse in a bed, on a sofa, or in a coffin at home.

Word spreads and mourners come at all hours to pray over the corpse, offer their condolences to the family. The house fills, empties and fills again. More people can see you dead than you ever knew in life.

Neighbours, usually women, help out in the kitchen making tea and sandwiches for the sets of wake-goers, who come and go. Drinks are served, prayers are said, and a squad of watchers, a quorum as old as the fall of Troy, sit ready to wake through the night with the corpse.

Why did our ancestors wake with their dead? Why did they feel the need to hold vigil over their indifferent dead, closer than the vigil we hold over a sick child? What is the purpose of fighting sleep on an uncomfortable hard-backed seat, the worst plane journey of your life, to guard an indifferent corpse from harm?

The core of the ritual is centred on two closely inter-twined cycles of change, the two most important existen-tial cycles of change in our existence: the cycle of the sun and the cycle of life.

———————

A wake in its simplest definition is a vigil over a dead body lasting through the night through one or two full solar cycles, day, night, day. The living stand guard over the dead to fulfil a set of ancient obligations between them-selves and both past and future dying generations.

The most important obligation is the recognition that this death is a death of one of Us, a fellow mortal, who must be properly laid to rest and not condemned to the eternal torment of the unburied.

Implicit in the same obligation is the social recognition of the pain and grief of the deceased's family, their loss. The living gather around the bereaved to play out these set rituals and help bind up the wound of mortality.

A manifestation of concern, of mortal love.

The wake is both an annunciation, the deadness of the deceased, and a rite of burial, a therapeutic rite of closure. A wake is also a stage, a liminal rite, where the forces of life and death contend for dominance.

Somewhere in the long hours of darkness after death our ancestors believed a portal opened between the living world and the afterlife for the fleeing soul to make safe passage. The boundaries between the natural and super-natural world were broken open.

Nor was the portal just one way. Once opened hordes of the unquiet dead could breach the door, escape from Hades, and reign in chaos on Earth again. The living had to gather around that portal, wake through the watches of the night and shore up the breach.

The dead had to stay dead and could never be allowed to return again to overthrow the natural world. The danger passes when that other existential cycle begins again and the life-giving sun rises in victory again at dawn.

It could be easy to dismiss such beliefs as superstitions until you talk to the recently bereaved where the reappearance of their loved ones in dreams for months, sometimes years, after their death is a common psychological grief reaction.

Why would you not believe such apparitions in the dreams of night-time, when the dead again walked the Earth, were not a message from the afterlife?

Sitting up all night though in the company of the dead on a hard chair is still a sacrifice. Why bother?

In Irish there is a word, *meitheal*, for a form of cooperative working between neighbours where individuals lend their labour, saving one farmer's summer crop in one day, and in turn receive the same benefit at some future date.

When I was a child on the island my grandfather's hay, for feeding the animals in the winter, was always harvested on one such day in a furious burst of energy with the help of such a *meitheal* of neighbours.

A *meitheal*, the opposite of everyone for their self, relies on trust and faith in others to fulfil their social obligation, a web of connection across a community.

A wake is a transcendent *meitheal*, a giving of oneself in the now in the hope that others, some as yet unborn, within the same community will fulfil these same duties at the hour of your own death. That when your time comes you too will be given a rite of burial and properly laid to rest. An act of faith.

It is the same *meitheal* that underlies the honour of carrying the coffin to the grave; for just as I carry the coffin of my mortal brother or sister today so too will I be carried by my brothers in a future time to come.

Together we are greater than our selves alone and can achieve so much more, gathering a harvest, raising a building, or binding up the wounds of grief, sorrow or trauma. Sharing the burden.

In the same togetherness, the Wake is its own lesson in taming our individual death fear. The Wake binds the living in a familiar rite, repeated and repeated, one dead body after another, until there is nothing strange about the sight of dry ice-cold remains.

Or your own death to come. Together we shall conquer death.

The Wake can also be an act of sexual renewal among the living. Sometimes the corpse, the very metre clock of Us, is an incitement for joy, sexual rebellion and the pleasures of sorrow of another kind.

The hungers of the living never stop so a wake always has food, drink, feasting and an uninhibited outpouring of emotion. A strong sexual undercurrent, a physical compulsion to have sex in defiance of death, is never far from expressing itself.

Irish Wakes were sometimes raucous libidinous gatherings where strong drink was consumed in quantity and trials of strength between male mourners and sexual play were orchestrated by a male jester figure called a Borekeen.

The Borekeen, an ancient pagan role, was a Dionysian figure inciting his followers in ritual madness, sexual ecstasy to create a new generation of sons and daughters and overcome death. Mock marriages, mock confessionals, and ancient wake games to encourage coupling, all within sight of the corpse, were common.

When I was a teenager on the island, I found myself playing just such a wake game, The Ring, one night, ten feet from a corpse. The Ring was a simple Spin-the-Bottle of sexual forfeits whose implicit aim was to overcome gawky teenage shyness and match you with a girlfriend or boyfriend.

The coldness of the corpse was a perverse aphrodisiac. There in the box old and wizened was our own distant fate but what mattered now was our animal hunger.

If you lost the round you were compelled to go outside into the dark with a girl or boy chosen for you by the Borekeen for five minutes – an ideal way of encouraging a teenage romance.

Why not mock the dead for soon enough we will join them?

The Ring, played out in teenage sniggers among the company of other aged mourners, had, although we never knew it, a deeper purpose. Playing such a wake game, in the company of a corpse, was just another way of taking the weight of our mortality and taming death.

I wonder if these Irish Wake games sound too much like history, quaint. Something that would never work in today's America, your English neighbourhood – where you don't even know who your next-door neighbour is and there are no communities left to gather and grieve together with.

But if you are thinking like that, you are thinking dead wrong.

We can't all return to the west coast of Ireland and live and die in the gatherings of a full-scale Irish Wake. But we can easily carry the lessons of 'taking the weight', being part of a volunteer *meitheal*, to our cities of glass, concrete and brick.

We can all use the small powers we do have, the phone in your pocket, to reconnect and recreate these ancient bonds. Instead of the shunning, we can reach out to the Other around us and offer ourselves to play a part in the visiting of the sick, bearing witness with the dying, even the carrying of the coffin. Speak out, offer our sorrow and condolences, and connect.

You don't have to worry about getting it right first time or even on the tenth time. Turning up, being present, is in itself a small act of intertwining between the living and the dead, a blessing.

To be truly human is to carry the burden of your own mortality and strive in grace, to help others carry theirs, sometimes lightly and sometimes courageously.

RULE NINE: LIVE EVERY DAY LIKE A WEDNESDAY.

RULE NINE

There would not be much point hanging out with the dead if it did not help you change your own life for the better. Help you lead a fuller more integrated life.

No one, unless they are sadly suicidal, volunteers to die. But finding the balance, the right way to live with death is not straightforward. We struggle.

There is always someone piously intoning on daytime TV that you've 'got to live your life like every day was your last.'

Carpe Diem.

It is an impossible burden.

We construct our lives, our selves, bit by bit: organising the shopping next weekend, going to work tomorrow, planning your summer holiday, having children and paying off the mortgage. Getting the washing machine fixed.

In order to live purposefully we have to believe in some

kind of future, some sort of ordinary becoming that is not too fearfully different from the present. Sort of like Wednesdays.

Wednesdays are the days of in-between things. The undefined middle. Long past the aftermath of last weekend, the Monday morning return to work, but too early for the expectation of the oncoming Friday night fireworks. Definitely not the Big Event.

Plot-wise, Wednesdays are never set down as the day for Armageddon by gods, novelists or Hollywood screenwriters. As these things go, Wednesdays are generally flat, unheralded. Workaday. Or Workanight.

Train schedules generally run smoother. Traffic, which cannot be snarled up because of the coming holiday weekend, flows. Coups don't happen. Marriages are rarely consummated. Does anyone ever move house on a Wednesday? Or dress up especially? Can you even remember what you were doing last Wednesday?

Wednesdays are wonderfully unimportant. We have long forgotten even who the day is named after, the Norse god Odin whose name was translated in Old English as Woden or Wotan eventually giving us Wödenesdaeg, Wednesday.

And that is good.

There is no expectation about 'having to get it done' by first thing on Wednesday. Wednesdays generally pass us by unremarked. Neither a beginning nor ending. More of a 'getting-through-the-week' sort of day.

Thankfully, corporate restaurant chains never trade-mark their restaurants TGIW – Thank God It's Wednesday.

But maybe we should in small ways celebrate Wednesdays more because they are just so ordinary, so authentic.

Wednesdays are go-home nights, eat in, pasta, stew, watch TV, sleep nights. Read in bed, get ready for the next day sort of thing, part of the ongoing. Wednesdays are homework nights. Or netball practice. Catching up on the ironing. The days when we stop pretending to be some-one else for other people.

Never the showdown, the showcase, or the parade. The who we are, not the image. The day when it is, and this is important, okay just to be you.

Wednesdays, as John Lennon said, are the sort of days when life happens as you are busy making other plans. When parcels are delivered, children born, exams passed, dates planned and joy comes unexpectedly. Or the same day when the wrong sort of test results come back from your doctor on that biopsy. Or the D-word, death, comes unexpected.

Could there ever be a good day to die? Or is our instinc-tive answer – no.

Never.

Never?

But that is the problem. The Never-problem. Because one day Never will turn into a Tuesday or a Saturday. Or a Sunday. Your Dying Day. As if from nowhere.

So later hopefully rather than sooner we are all going to have to answer the question anyway.

Which would be the best day for me to die?

Yes, but what about my children, my family? My cat? All the people I would leave behind?

The life to come? The things left undone? The apartment? The plants? I haven't even written a will.

I would have only lived half my life.

Half your life?

When we do think of death, we want to believe there is some sort of natural order in the world; begotten, born, live happily to an old age, then die quick. And in the rich West if statistics were all that mattered then we would be roughly right, though you are far more likely to die slow of multiple degenerative disease conditions. But when it comes to the individual statistic of You, believing in your future uninterruptable decades of life and absolute certainty of retirement plans is just more delusional thinking.

Death comes when it comes. At the traffic light. The neighbourhood barbecue. Somewhere even in the panic of a viral pandemic. Next Monday might be the day. Or some Friday next month. Or the second Wednesday of the third month the year after. And that will be your Life. Or the life of someone you love.

I remember once being on holiday in Greece and we went to a beach restaurant on the sand and sat under an umbrella in a blazing sun and ate fresh sardines on a white linen tablecloth and drank cold frosted-up-outside-of-the-bottle-dripping-with-condensation white wine.

It was a great day and everyone at the table was happy. All the worries of the world were far away and I was happy too.

And in between courses if you wanted to you could dive into a delicious cooling sea, swim for a bit, then sit back in the chair at the table, let the salt dry on your skin and eat something else like octopus.

Then later on it got dark and I went back to the house where I was staying close to the same beach, had sex with someone I loved, and fell asleep listening to the sound of the waves on the shore and the children breathing through the open door in the adjacent room.

It could have been a good day to die but I am glad it wasn't.

I was in my thirties and had lots of other things I wanted to do in life and some of them I even managed to do like writing this book. And some of them I haven't. And maybe never will. For three decades I worked as a reporter and film-maker in some troubled lands: Northern Ireland, Iran, Afghanistan, Israel, Gaza, Africa. Wars, famines, plagues.

Death was closer. Every day. Hospitals full of dying AIDS patients. Rooms filled with gunmen who smiled and laughed even though they had planted car bombs in crowded streets, murdering hundreds, and had tortured countless others. Or kidnappers with their Kalashnikovs in the wilds of Afghanistan who sized you up for the potential ransom to be extracted.

One night I was coming out of a small Palestinian village in the West Bank and I and my Palestinian driver got stopped at an Israeli army checkpoint. Just the two of us. It was real dark and we were alone in the middle of nowhere on the road home to Jerusalem.

We showed our IDs and let the soldier search the car where he found my reporter's flak jacket in the boot. For some reason the soldier doing the checking went crazy angry, pointed his rifle towards us and threatened to kill us. He took the flak jacket out of the car as if he was going to steal it, dragged it around and threw it inside his checkpoint. None of his actions made sense. A flak jacket is something you wear as a reporter to stop other people killing you with their guns and we were unarmed. But we were not in a strong position to argue.

We asked politely if he would radio his commanders to check out our IDs and let us through the checkpoint but he pointed his rifle at us again and said he would shoot us if we moved.

It is a scary moment in the dark when someone with a

gun is screaming in a foreign language that he is going to kill you. And you are just waiting for the bullets to come through the side of the car and end your life.

We were trapped, powerless. There was no one to call for help; my editors back in London and my family were beyond reach. I didn't want to die there on the side of the road in the dark.

It did not feel like a good day to die either.

I never got shot. We sat in the car and then my friend, my driver, made some calls to some human rights organisations who made some calls to the Israel Defense Forces and, eventually, the angry soldier was forced to return the flak jacket and let us go.

And soon, less than an hour, I was back in my hotel in Jerusalem sipping a beer, watching the laughter on the faces of other diners, letting the fear slip away from me into the darkness of the terrace feeling pleased.

I never lost half my life and I am glad. But, of course, getting shot dead at an Israeli checkpoint could so easily have been my day to die.

Or being knocked down walking innocently by the side of the road in some common town.

Or falling down the stairs in your own home.

Or getting the dog lead entangled in the bike's front wheel on a quiet country road and then slamming your head into the stone kerb and dying of a brain haemorrhage.

Or a thousand other small mortal happenstances.

Life is not a contest, a journey or a certainty. Life is a responsibility.

This is the only life we will ever have and we will define our lives every day in the actions we undertake. How we act. How we have created ourselves. How we define ourselves too in the universal Us.

Just as we define ourselves too in those ordinary Wednesdays of the days of our lives in those thousands of small obligations, recognitions, kindnesses or cruelties towards our fellow mortals.

Given that we will never have the choice of when the day comes the one thing we can do is concentrate on the responsibilities. Our responsibilities.

Did I want my life? This life? Am I proud of me and my part in the mortal Us?

Would this be a good day to die?

And if this was my day to die, my Wednesday, would I be okay with today?

———————

The world is full of guides about How-to-Be.

How to Get Richer, Sleep with More People, Be Happier, Be More Successful, Win More Followers. Their underlying message is that you can change the world by your individual will.

Rise to the top of the pile on the seabed, straighten your shoulders and become the Alpha Lobster. Mate with more female lobsters and have a bigger car, a bigger house and a Bigger Happiness. Who would not want an easier life?

And so we judge, compare ourselves, all the time, so many clicks, so many followers, so much money, so much attention. We are lured up by the shiny, the new, the bright.

A flimsy hierarchy of TV stars, thought leaders, politicians and fashion gurus whose presence fills the current stage but whose real impact on our lives is best tangential, at worse irrelevant.

Advertising copy to help sell more household goods.

In the company of the dead it is impossible not to question your own route to happiness.

Or silence – the why. Why am I doing this? Reading this? Watching this? Wasting my life on this?

Set against the ice-cold touch of a corpse, does it ever matter who won what so-called celebrity trophy?

Or is that just the white noise we use to fill a hole inside ourselves?

All the time we edit out what we perceive as failure or the forgotten: the girl bands who never quite became stars, the political gods of yesteryear and last year's prophets. The losing side of whatever World Series we cheer for. The glow of their seamless replacements never fades.

But death teaches something else.

That the universe is full of ordinary lives, your grand-mother, your uncle, your colleague, your son and daughter. Yourself.

How are we to rate their lives? And our own? What is truly meaningful about being alive?

For every shining star there are a lot of other same stars that once glittered with just about the same brightness in the same firmament but never got chosen.

Just because you want something or something to be, even when you follow the drill, doesn't make it happen. Or devalue the worth of the endeavour or the life that aspired.

Sometimes if we are lucky, we think we get to be the thing we want to be. And sometimes we don't.

Power, privilege, the way the world is, all play a part. Then there is talent, hard work and chance. The road turns towards whatever we define as fortune. A lot of the time though it doesn't. It is not a fault or a failure, just a life outcome.

Sometimes we destroy ourselves on the road. Sometimes the destruction happens beyond our will. And sometimes we let other people do the destroying for us. A lot of times we are powerless to change the world and its order.

Nor is everyone called upon to be a hero or change history or do much more than live a life of small kind-nesses and quiet dignity.

Generally the world gets better one dental appointment at a time, one small problem solved, one further lesson taught, after another.

Other lives, sometimes our lives, through no fault of their own are lived out fraught with hardships and poverty.

Most of us will live the life we have to lead, often because there is no other choice.

Power wanes, glories fade. Does anyone know off the top of their head who won the Oscar in 1998? Or 2010? And who was the Secretary of State for Business then? Or who won the Premier League that year too?

As it turns out politicians, sport stars, the rich and famous are just as mortal, just as forgettable, as the rest of us.

Death because it is truly universal forces us to re-question the pathway we can lead in our own lives, the endless going on.

Can we remember to live just being ourselves?

Learn to respect the integrity of our own life? And then see the same value in the lives and deaths of all or any of those ordinary mortals around us. The Others, the Us, and their connection with our own lives? Or are we still entranced by the shiny brightness of the seemingly new, the shimmering ephemeral?

Maybe we too don't have many real choices about where we live, our job, the money we earn, our relationships but we can all still make small different choices about how we live our life.

How we connect to other people.

How we do death, other people's deaths, tells us a lot about us. The who we really are. The mortal kinship we all share.

Remembering to live is also a pretty good incentive to remember to enjoy yourself.

I like cooking seafood for my family, and oysters and champagne, and going to foreign countries to see the lives of others, the journey to Troy, and reading books.

Everyone wants different things. The world is full of wonder and part of the joy and fear is that you won't have the next three hundred years to get to go on honeymoon to Zanzibar or Rhode Island. Or run away to the circus. Or go on a pilgrimage. Or sit at home making stew. Or wherever or whatever you want.

But it's better to try and do it now or nowish because you really will not get the chance to do it when you are dead, and if you've read this far then you will know you can never be sure when you actually will be dead.

Nothing lasts and neither do we so seize the days, weeks or years for what you want.

Your life now is your own responsibility, how you act, your part in that mortal Us, your recognition of the value, the humanity, of the other lives around you.

And your death too.

EPILOGUE: NINE RULES TO CONQUER DEATH

EPILOGUE

Is that it? **Nine Rules?**

Pretty much. So be nicer to other people? See dead bodies. Touch them? Go to more funerals.

And eat more seafood?

Follow the **Nine Rules?**

Not really.

By now you should see the trick, the sleight of hand: that the only way to conquer death is to embrace it by reaching out to the community of mortals all around you. To lessen your own mortal burden by sharing the burdens of others. To volunteer and take part in the transcendent *meitheal* between the living and the dead in all the other lives around you. To take the weight.

There are no shortcuts to overcoming our death fear. But you still do have the real choice about what sort of mortal you want to be.

NINE RULES TO CONQUER DEATH

Good. Bad. Fearful.

The big simple lesson of the Irish Wake, seeing the dead in the company of your community, is about reaching out, integrating a little bit of death into your life and feeling more relaxed about dying, about being mortal. Being human.

It's about leaning into your mortality and letting go of your fears by helping others with their fears. And leading a fuller life as your own mortal self.

It is about recognising the real music of your own life amidst the noise around you. Your own life song. The difference between the ephemeral and the essential.

And what could be more essential than learning to conquer death?

The very worst thing that could possibly happen is that you die. But hopefully you won't be alone.

We cannot all go back to the west coast of Ireland, listen to the daily radio, and go out every other day to a full-scale Irish Wake. Stay up all night waking the dead.

But then you don't really need to. All you need to do is apply the **Nine Rules**, or your own version of them, whenever you hear of another mortal in pain.

The choice is always your own.

Do you reach out to connect, overcome your fear and recognise your own humanity in the sick, the dying and the dead?

Or do you raise your hands to your ears to drown out

the sound of these others' keening and quickly pass on by to disconnect yourself?

Learning to be mortal, even to be a better mortal, is not just something you can do in a few hours. In fact even with the **Nine Rules** on your phone it is going to take you a lifetime of practice to get right.

But once you get the hang of the simple rules and act upon them then, like our foremothers and fathers, you will be ready to endure both the worst and the best days of life. As they did on the plans of Nineveh, in Troy, in Rome and in the wild bogs of Ireland's Atlantic seaboard for thousands of years.

Learning how to do death will make you: wiser, more patient, more resilient, stronger, more sympathetic. The rules show you how to live and be a better human.

Rule One: Being mortal is the one thing in life you don't get to choose.
Rule Two: If we did not die life would be terrible.
Rule Three: Pretending you are immortal is a bad idea.
Rule Four: Nothing much changes under the mortal sun.
Rule Five: Learning how to die is the same as learning how to live.
Rule Six: The dead are everything and nothing like Us.

Rule Seven: The pleasure of the sorrow of tears.
Rule Eight: Take the weight.
Rule Nine: Live every day like a Wednesday.

Whether we wish for it or not, we are all part of the mortal Us and we will define ourselves, in courage or cowardice, in recognition or denial, in our own mortality, our universal kinship, in the lives and deaths of others.

I die, you die. But we still have a choice. Do we die alone in fear, lost among strangers?

Or do we die within a community who hold us close and see, no matter how far from greatness, their own dying brother, their own dying sister, their own dying self, worthy too of the same respect, for being just human, just mortal, as we are?

Do you recognise yourself as part of that community?

Do you want to be human?

You don't need to be Irish to follow the rulebook of the Irish Wake, you just need to be ready to overcome your death fear, and reach out into the lives, the dyings and deaths going on all around to offer your support, affirmation, and yourself, as one of the mortal Us.

Because we have temporarily lost our way with death you might need to steel yourself at first with a bit of death courage to overcome your fear and learn again how to conquer death.

But after a few wakes and corpses and funerals you'll be surprised how easy death is to talk about like it is the most natural thing in the world.

And that dying is just part of life. Your life too.

May you die in grace, surrounded by those you love, on a good day.

ACKNOWLEDGEMENTS

Books are acts of faith. And that first act of faith is grounded in the belief of others that the hours of devotion to the computer screen are a worthy use of time. I would like to thank River, Savanna and Storme for their patience. And Dea, the biggest faith keeper of all.

We carry our dead with us so this work is the result of many journeys, and many sharings by other lives. I am eternally grateful to those others for their life courage in sharing.

And for my mothers' and fathers' island and its peoples who have since my first wake at seven taught so much about life, death and courage.

I am grateful too to the boy, that distant stranger, who in valour stepped out blind on the road alone, so many decades ago, believing the journey itself was worthy of the endeavour.

And for those who get there I hope you all enjoy the sight of Halley's Comet in the night skies as I never will.